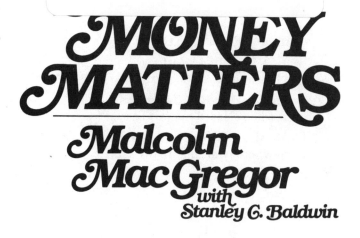

MONEY MATTERS

Malcolm MacGregor

with
Stanley C. Baldwin

*A CPA's sometimes humorous,
consistently practical guide
to personal money management,
based on Scripture and with an
emphasis on family living.*

BETHANY HOUSE PUBLISHERS
Minneapolis, Minnesota 55438

DEDICATED TO:

Rev. Jack Mathews,
who challenged me to ministry,

My pastor, Rev. Jerry Cook,
who released my ministry,

and Meg, Greg, George and Margaret Mary,
all of whom come before my ministry

This edition, updated 1988

Scripture quotations are from the King James version and the New American Standard Bible (NASB).

Published by Bethany House Publishers
A Division of Bethany Fellowship, Inc.
6820 Auto Club Road, Minneapolis, Minnesota 55438

Printed in the United States of America

Library of Congress Cataloging-in-Publication Data

MacGregor, Malcolm, 1945-
    Your money matters.

    1. Finance, Personal.   I. Baldwin, Stanley C., joint author.
II. Title.
HG179.M23   332'.024   76-56123
ISBN 0-87123-662-1

Preface

October 29, 1987

It was on this date 58 years ago that the stock market crash ushered in the Great Depression. The events of the last two weeks, however, have caused us to wonder—could it happen again?

As I review the preface from seven years ago, I find myself wondering at how the average family can make it. As a matter of fact, one article I read recently suggests that the middle class family is actually worse off today than they were in 1972.

The consumer price index stands at 344.4. This means that goods and services that cost $100 in 1967 now cost $344.40. Just seven years ago, the index was 244.9. Translated to wages, this means you now need to be earning in excess of $35,000 a year to have the same purchasing power that $25,000 had in 1980.

Budget cuts have caused the Bureau of Labor Statistics to stop publishing the urban family budget. Their typical family of four needed $23,594 a year to maintain a moderate standard of living in June of 1980. The budget assumed home ownership, a car three years old, meat at least once a day, eating out occasionally—certainly not overly luxurious! Using the rise in CPI, I estimate that it would take about $33,434 to live at this level in 1987. Since the median family income in 1986 was $29,458, I conclude that less than half of you can even think about this moderate lifestyle!

The $40 billion deficit we had budgeted in 1981 wasn't enough by almost $180 billion. Our record budget deficits for the past seven years, coupled with our record trade deficits, have put us in the position of a debtor nation for the first time in this century.

I am more convinced than ever that living a debt-free life according to God's principles is the only way to prepare for what is likely to be a very rough decade in the 90s. Good luck!

Malcolm MacGregor

Contents

Acknowledgments

The authors wish to acknowledge their indebtedness to Bill Gothard for principles gleaned from his seminars, and to George M. Bowman for concepts suggested by his book, *How to Succeed With Your Money* (Moody Press).

MALCOLM D. MacGREGOR is a Certified Public Accountant with offices in Gresham, Oregon. He is a former Controller of Stockman's Life Insurance Company of America and a former senior examiner with the State of Oregon Insurance Division. Increasingly, Mr. MacGregor is giving his energies to conducting money management seminars for local church congregations.

STANLEY C. BALDWIN is an author, editor, and Bible teacher residing near Oregon City, Oregon. He is the co-author of *The Kink and I*, and has written *What Did Jesus Say About That?* and *What Makes You So Special?* In addition, he has been a contributor to *Christianity Today, Moody Monthly* and *Eternity* magazines. He currently serves as president of the Oregon Association of Christian Writers and teaches writing on the college level.

PART I

Understanding What Causes
Money Problems

1

Seven Major Money Mistakes and How To Avoid Them

Suppose you and I could enter homes unnoticed and listen to the disputes of husbands and wives. We'd find that a surprisingly large percentage of those unpleasant words would revolve around money.

We drop into Home Number 1 just in time to hear her say, "Money, money, money! That's all you ever think about."

"Well, the way you spend it, you'd better be happy that *someone* in this family thinks about it," he replies.

We move quickly to Home Number 2 and hear, "If you and your brother hadn't gotten involved in that shaky land scheme, we wouldn't be in this mess. According to you, this deal was supposed to put us on Easy Street, not in bankruptcy court."

"Okay, okay," he replies, "now throw that in my face again. I make one mistake trying to provide security for you and the kids and you never let me live it down."

At House Number 3 we hear, "I thought you said you paid the Crackdown Credit Collection agency this month. I get pretty tired of having to smooth-talk collectors just because you never can pay on time."

"Well, the next time he calls tell him to drop dead; I'll pay that bill when I get around to it. Now cheer up. Here, look at this snazzy new tape deck I bought for the boat. It was only $11 down and $11 a month."

I hope such conversations don't strike close to your home, but unfortunately they are typical of many conversations being carried on right now. I can say this with certainty because I've been involved in enough counseling situations to know. These conversations reflect violations of basic principles of finance that are outlined in the Bible. Principles that, when followed, guarantee success—and when not followed, just as surely, guarantee trouble.

There are seven major money mistakes all too common in our society today: debt, irresponsibility, wrong values, speculation, selfishness, cheating, and wrong priorities. Let me briefly describe each of these.

1. *Getting into Debt*

You load 16 tons, and what do you get?
Another day older and deeper in debt.
St. Peter, don't you call me 'cause I can't go,
I owe my soul to the company store.

That old miner's song expresses the futility and frustration of a person held in economic slavery in a company town. Under that system in its worst forms, a whole town was owned by its single local industry. The workers were grossly underpaid but couldn't quit because there was no place else in town to work. And there was no money to help them move elsewhere. The small wage they did receive was taken for "services rendered" by the company. It owned the housing and charged high rent for sub-standard living quarters. It also owned the store and charged high prices for food and commodities. This system kept people in economic bondage even though slavery had been abolished years before.

Today you can get into a comparable position. You can be exploited economically and kept per-petually poor simply by allowing yourself to get into debt.

I do not believe that God wants His people to be in debt. Scripture tells us, "The borrower is ser-vant to the lender" (Prov. 22:7). Any time we incur debt we assume a servant relationship to our cred-itor because we must now work for him to pay our debt. God tells us not to become a servant to any man, but instead to serve Christ (see 1 Cor. 7:21-23). So, debt is bad, first, because it tends to *disqualify* us from serving the Lord. Joe can't answer God's call to train for the ministry because he has debts he must work to pay.

Jill can't teach in Vacation Bible School or be active in home Bible studies or even stay home to care for her own children because both she and her husband must work to help pay family debts.

Debt not only disqualifies people but it also *dis-tresses* them.

Too many of us have felt the distress of the heavy pressure of debt. We add up all our bills at month's end, and they come to $1,640. We look at available income and it's $1,500. We say, "O Lord, where am I going to get the $140?" It's not there.

God knew the type of pressure that debt could put on us, and He did not want us to be involved in it. So His Word says, "Owe no man any thing" (Rom. 13:8). He makes one exception: our debt of love. That's the only debt we are to be constantly paying on and never pay in full.

Debt is *discouraging* too. It's no fun to pay and pay for something you already have. And it's downright depressing to look ahead at months or even years of payments before you can call your income your own.

Debt also *divides* husbands and wives. He comes home from work, and she doesn't have dinner ready. She wants to go out to eat. He says, "We can't afford it. Can't you understand that?"

She says, "No, we can *never* afford to go out for dinner, but you could afford to spend $25 on a fishing trip last weekend."

"Great," he says; "I go on one fishing trip the whole year just to get my nose away from the grindstone for a little while, and I never hear the last of it."

"Well, when am I supposed to get a break?" she says. "You never think about that." And she starts crying.

Believe me, you can do without disqualifying, distressing, discouraging, divisive debt. And much of the subsequent content of this book is designed to show you how.

2. *Irresponsible Use of Resources*

God entrusts each of us with certain resources, and He expects us to be good stewards of what we have.

A principle emphasized repeatedly in Scripture is that if we do well in using limited resources, we will receive more; but if we misuse what little we have, even that will be taken from us. This is such an important principle that Jesus devoted two of His parables to it: the parables of the pounds (Luke 19:11-26) and of the talents (Matt. 25:14-30).

There are many ways to waste resources and bring poverty upon yourself. We have already mentioned one: *incurring debt.* When you incur debt, a sizable proportion of your money goes for interest and carrying charges. You end up paying more and receiving less.

Another irresponsible use of resources is indulging in *impulse buying.* You see something and you want it, so you buy it. You haven't checked the quality of the product. You haven't compared prices. You haven't determined what other costs may be involved in keeping and using the item.

I have developed a checklist of eleven questions to ask about proposed purchases. This safeguard system against impulse buying is discussed in detail in the chapter entitled "How To Recognize a Good Buy When You See It."

A third way people waste resources is by *careless management.* This carelessness can take two forms: first, inattention to one's money; and second, neglect of one's property.

Many people are careless about their money. They don't pay much attention to how they are spending it. Their typical cry is: "Where did it all go?" Husband says to wife, "What, you're out of money already? I just gave you $80; where did it go?"

She says, "Well, let's see, I spent almost $22 last night at the grocery store, and I gave Junior $5 for lunch money this week, and . . . oh, yes, it was $18.50 for these cute shoes I got on sale."

Her computer-minded husband, adding in his head while she has been talking, replies, "Okay, that's $45.50; what happened to the other $34.50?"

The way to avoid this kind of scene is to have a budget and to keep a record of all expenses. Later we will discuss budgeting in full detail. For now, remember the old adage: *If you are going to manage your assets properly, you don't ask where the money went; you tell it where to go.*

The second form of irresponsibility, neglect of one's property, has no better description than in the ancient account of wise King Solomon:

I passed by the field of the sluggard,
And by the vineyard of the man lacking sense;
And behold, it was completely overgrown with thistles,
Its surface was covered with nettles,
And its stone wall was broken down.
When I saw, I reflected upon it;
I looked, and received instruction.
"A little sleep, a little slumber
A little folding of the hands to rest,"
Then your poverty will come as a robber,
And your want like an armed man.

(Prov. 24:30-34, NASB)

To put it in blunt contemporary terms, if you are too lazy to take care of your property, if you allow your house, your yard, your car to deteriorate because of neglect or abuse, you impoverish yourself.

3. *A Money-Centered Life*

In 1921, nine of the world's most successful money-making businessmen got together at the Edgewater Hotel in Chicago. They included the head of the greatest monopoly, the most successful speculator on Wall Street, the president of the largest independent steel company, the president of the largest utility company, the president of the largest gas company, the greatest wheat speculator in the United States, the president of the New York Stock Exchange, the president of the Bank of International Settlements, and a member of the president's cabinet. These men were implicated in the Teapot Dome Scandal.

Twenty-five years later, where were these men of fantastic wealth and power? Ivar Krueger, head of the greatest monopoly, died of suicide. Jessie Livermore, the most successful speculator on Wall Street, died of suicide. Charles Schwab, president of the largest independent steel company, died in bankruptcy and lived on borrowed money for five years before his death. Samuel Insull, the president of the greatest utility company, died a fugitive from the law, penniless, in a foreign land. Howard Hopson, president of the largest gas company, went insane. Arthur Cotton, the greatest wheat speculator, died abroad, bankrupt. Richard Whitney, president of the New York Stock Exchange, was finally released from Sing Sing Penitentiary. Leon Frasier, president of the Bank of International Settlements, died of suicide. Albert Fall, member of the president's cabinet, was pardoned from prison so he could die at home.

What's the moral of that little story? Well, it could be that money can't bring happiness, but on the other hand these men may have been very happy while they had money. Perhaps it is that riches are transient; it's difficult to keep them. But some families do so for generations. It was probably the crash of the stock market in 1929 and the subsequent Great Depression that wiped out most or all of the men in our story.

The real point of the story is that when their money went, so did they. The sun kept shining, the flowers kept blooming, and multitudes of common people took in their belts a bit and went on living, but these men were destroyed. Why? Because they had centered their lives in money, and when it was gone, they had nothing to live for.

Jesus said, "Take heed, and beware of covetousness, for a man's life consisteth not in the abundance of the things which he possesseth" (Luke 12:15). It's easy to forget that and to become so preoccupied with making money or accumulating possessions that our life amounts to little else.

By contrast, the attitude we *should* have is also described by Scripture. "But godliness with contentment is great gain. For we brought nothing into this world, and it is certain we can carry nothing out. And having food and raiment let us be therewith content" (1 Tim. 6:6-8).

Rich people are by no means the only victims of the error of money-centered living. In fact, some rich people are less preoccupied with money and possessions than some poor people are. Scripture says:

> But they that will be rich [not "are rich"] fall into temptation and a snare, and into many foolish and hurtful lusts, which drown men in destruction and perdition. For *the love of money* [not "the possession of money"] is the root of all evil: which while some coveted after, they have erred from the faith, and pierced themselves through with many sorrows (1 Tim. 6:9-10).

So, even though this is a book about money, it should not lead you to be preoccupied with money. The section on "Strengthening the Family Through Right Use of Money" is an example of keeping some balance on the subject.

4. *Trying To "Get Rich Quick"*

The Scripture says, "He that hasteth to be rich hath an evil eye, and considereth not that poverty shall come upon him" (Prov. 28:22). What a dynamic verse! I have a mental picture of this guy with an evil gleam in his eye. He thinks he is really going to make a financial killing, but he's in for trouble.

So often we hear of grand schemes: "Invest $500 in this and in three weeks you're going to have $1000 profit. Two weeks later you'll have $2000 more profit, and in another month, $4000 profit. A couple of months after that you can take a vacation—go to the Bahamas—you'll have earned thousands of dollars at that point in time."

The guy pitching this line seems very successful. He leaves his Cadillac running the whole time he's talking to you because money is no object to him.

You think, *Wow! Here's my opportunity, and opportunity knocks only once. I've got to invest in this.* You have a garage sale and sell everything that's not nailed down. You hock your wife's rings, borrow all you can from her folks, and go zipping on back with the money. You really are into this thing.

Often these schemes require getting other people involved in the business venture with you, and then you are making money off their efforts. They in turn get more people. Laws are being passed specifically restricting such "pyramids" because they have been so badly abused. People get involved and a few months later they get out, but they are not out of debt. If anything, they are probably further in debt trying to keep up the appearance of being successful.

"Discretion shall preserve thee, understanding shall keep thee" (Prov. 2:11). You need to be very discreet and understanding about money-making schemes. We also read twice in Proverbs that in a "multitude of counsellors there is safety" (11:14; 24:6). If someone comes to you with a business opportunity, you don't necessarily say no. Yes could be the right answer; but get some counsel from other people.

May I say as a professional involved with many beginning businessmen, it is rare to be able to earn a living wage any sooner than one year after you start a business. This is true not only of a brand-new business, but also of a branch of an existing business that has all sorts of advertising behind it. That is why, with many franchises, the financing arrangements actually involve underwriting your efforts for a period of time until your business becomes viable.

So be wary of quick and easy ways to get rich.

5. *Withholding Benevolence*

Two Bible principles that go together are giving and receiving. If you give, you will receive. Jesus said:

> Give, and it shall be given unto you; good measure, pressed down, and shaken together, and running over shall men give into your bosom. For with the same measure that ye mete withal it shall be measured to you again (Luke 6:38).

It's possible to give away and be richer, and it's possible to hold onto things and lose as a result. In the words of Scripture:

> There is one who scatters, yet increases all the more, and there is one who withholds what is justly due, but it results only in want. The generous man will be prosperous, and he who waters will himself be watered (Prov. 11:24-25, NASB).

This is such an important concept! We must be a giving people if ever we are to receive all God wants to give us.

Giving and receiving operates in three areas.

First, toward God: "Honour the Lord with thy sub-
stance, and with the firstfruits of all thine increase"
(Prov. 3:9). That's giving to God. And what does
the next verse say? "So shall thy barns be filled
with plenty, and thy presses shall burst out with
new wine" (v. 10). That's receiving.

"Bring ye all the tithes into the storehouse, that
there may be meat in mine house" (Mal. 3:10a).
That's giving to God. "And prove me now herewith,
saith the Lord of hosts, if I will not open you the
windows of heaven, and pour you out a blessing,
that there shall not be room enough to receive it"
(Mal. 3:10b). That's really receiving!

The second area for benevolence is toward other
Christians—helping one another. There is grace both
in giving and in receiving. God wants us all to be
involved in this. "As we have therefore opportunity,
let us do good unto all men, especially unto them
who are of the household of faith" (Gal. 6:10). It
is easy for some to give, but often much more difficult to receive. Pride is an issue here. But obviously
if Christians are to help fellow Christians in need,
the latter must have grace enough to receive the
help.

The third area for our benevolence is toward the
poor. John the Baptist preached, "He that hath two
coats, let him impart to him that hath none; and
he that hath meat, let him do likewise" (Luke 3:11).

Consider these gems of wisdom on the same subject from the book of Proverbs. "He that hath mercy
on the poor, happy is he" (14:21). "He that honoureth
him [God] hath mercy on the poor" (14:31). "He
that hath pity upon the poor lendeth unto the Lord
[giving]; and that which he hath given will he
pay him again [receiving]" (19:17).

My friend and collaborator Stanley Baldwin has

written on this subject in his excellent book *What Did Jesus Say About That?**

> People have all sorts of excuses for failing to help the poor. "It's their own fault; if they weren't so lazy—if they would get off their backsides and go to work—they wouldn't be poor," or, "I'm not helping those deadbeats; let them get theirs like I got mine."

> More subtle, but with the same effect, is the concern often expressed by Christians that a handout is demeaning, that it does more harm than good. Which all sounds reasonable, and perhaps it is. In certain situations, perhaps one should not give to the poor. But to make not giving the rule—well, you'll have to argue with Jesus about that! He's the One who said to give to the poor. Maybe He didn't understand people so well as you do?

Of course, Jesus did understand people. And He understood the importance of benevolence. We'll learn something more of its importance in succeeding chapters.

6. *Cheating*

Many people think of the business world as a dog-eat-dog place in which everybody is out to take everybody else. A cartoon I saw suggested that. A speaker was addressing a group of graduates, and as they were leaving the academic environment to face the realities of the business world, he told them, "I would like to mention that the honor system is no longer in effect."

Many men in business disagree. They will tell you that honesty is not just the best policy; it is the only policy for guaranteeing continued success.

Dishonesty may bring success for a while. The

---

* © Victor Books, Wheaton, Ill. Used by permission.

Bible tells us that. "A bribe works like magic. Whoever uses it will prosper" (Prov. 17:8, Living Bible). "A bribe does wonders; it will bring you before men of importance!" (Prov. 18:16, Living Bible). But it also says bribery is wrong. "A wicked man receives a bribe from the bosom to pervert the ways of justice" (Prov. 17:23, NASB).

Our society has experienced some tremendous upheavals from bribes. Some of our largest firms have bribed government officials in foreign lands in order to get favors and contracts and land rights. Ultimately, the truth came out and these people paid the penalty.

In the long run dishonesty will always harm you, even though the short-run profits may look enticing. I recently read a book called *The Great Train Robbery,* a fascinating account of a robbery in England in the 1850s. An old adage says, "Crime does not pay," but this crime did pay from the standpoint of dollars and cents in the thieves' pockets. Yet how do you measure dollars and cents in your pocket against a jail term of 15, 20, or 30 years? I can't reconcile that. There is not enough money in the world for which to trade my freedom. I'm set free in Christ, and He guarantees to meet my needs besides. That's unbeatable!

If I gain dishonestly, I'm going to be in trouble with God whether or not I am ever punished by man. James talks about rich men who cheat their laborers. He says that the cries of those who are cheated reach the ears of God (James 5:1). God is going to punish those who prosper by cheating others.

Apart from penalties for dishonesty, God's Word gives us an example of having "a conscience void of offence toward God, and toward man" (Acts 24:16). I want my record to be clean in this respect.

As Stanley Baldwin points out in his book cited earlier, Jesus taught that one of our basic aims should be to use our money to help others. When we cheat, he says, we

> exactly reverse Jesus' teaching. Instead of getting money to help people, we hurt people to get money. ... Whenever we wrong or hurt someone for material gain, whenever we cheat, we reveal that we are 180 degrees removed from the attitude toward money that Jesus said we should display.

I want to be with Jesus on this issue, not going exactly contrary to what He teaches. Don't you?

7. *The Business or Job-Oriented Life*

"As Christ's soldier do not let yourself become tied up in worldly affairs, for then you cannot satisfy the one who has enlisted you in his army" (2 Tim. 2:4, Living Bible). As men, we have a great desire to succeed. We get involved in our job or business and if we're not careful we become completely absorbed in it—"tied up" in it, as the Living Bible says.

Wholehearted endeavor is good. Yet we need to keep things in proper perspective: God first, family second, work third. The real root of our difficulties is that we don't keep things in proper perspective. Far too many Christians place work before family and before God. That's not God's way to success.

A man who has been in business for himself comes in to see me. A tremendous opportunity had come along. Once he got this business established, he was going to have a lot of time available to minister at the church and help others.

He had excitedly told his family that he had found an opportunity to be his own boss and to have the freedom he wanted. They must understand that for a short period of time he was going to have to pour a lot of work and time into getting the business started, but after that he would have a lot of extra time. He would be able to help out at church, perhaps coaching Little League, and they would do things together as a family.

So the very first thing he did was to resign his position on the church council, because, after all, the council met on Saturday and that was one day he *had* to be at work. It was his big day. But as soon as he got his business started, he'd be back.

Business was going well, but he was not coming to the midweek service anymore, for that was the night he needed to catch up on his book work. Then he quit his position as Sunday school teacher because he didn't have time to prepare his lesson properly. Next, he stopped coming to church on Sunday evening. Then a crisis set in, and he was not in church on Sunday mornings for six, eight, ten weeks.

Now, finally, he is sitting across the desk from me. His business is utterly destroyed and he's facing bankruptcy. He says, "Why would God put me into this business just to see it fail?"

Well, I'm not so sure God put him there to begin with, but it's clear that he didn't have things in proper perspective.

Keeping our priorities straight is so difficult. I probably blow it more times than not, but I am glad for the times when I've come through.

One Saturday my son was involved in the Cub Scout Olympics. I had arranged my schedule so that I would be at the games in the morning, and in the afternoon I would take care of two business appointments. These were important appointments, one involving some tax audits. I showed up at the designated time for the Cub Scout Olympics and was informed that we had been given the wrong time and they wouldn't start until 2 o'clock.

I was about to tell my son that I couldn't attend because I had business appointments at 2 and 3:30, and I just had to be there. I looked at him and I knew he wanted me there. The thought flashed through my mind: *God first, family second, business third.*

I telephoned the two men with whom I had appointments and explained to them that I could not come and that we would have to make other arrangements. They were both rather upset with me. One was planning to be out of town and couldn't meet later. Both were so displeased that they were talking about changing accountants, which was their right.

I said, "Lord, I'm doing what I think is right. I'm putting you first and then my family before my business. Please honor this decision."

As it turned out, the first man's partner came over later that afternoon with information that completely changed the approach on the tax audit, which meant our hour and a half would have been totally wasted. The second man's brother called him from the airport. They had not seen one another since the brother had accepted the Lord three years before. He had only this chance to go out to the airport and spend four hours with his brother, have dinner, and share the life in Jesus. The time of the airport trip? About 3:30.

Both of these men called me on Monday and apologized. They said they recognized that as a Christian brother my commitment to my family was solid and had to be first. The incident caused them to reexamine their own priorities.

God will honor you if you put Him first, your family second, your job third, rather than letting your work so totally occupy your mind and your life that you're not able to live the way God intended.

There certainly are other mistakes often made with regard to money, but these seven are the major ones. We'll point out some others as we go along. Now let's focus on the positive side.

What can you do that's right? How can you manage your finances in a positive and responsible way that God will bless? That will be our emphasis from here on.

PART II

Laying a Foundation for Financial Freedom

2

Settle the Ownership Question

Did you see yourself in chapter 1?

If you are anything like the people who sit in my seminars, I'm sure you did. I notice people literally wincing as I mention some of these major mistakes. Sometimes I see a wife give her husband the elbow, or the two look knowingly at each other.

Perhaps you haven't made every one of the seven major money mistakes mentioned in chapter 1, but you're a rare person if you haven't made any of them. Now you know what to avoid, so you are all set to build a solid structure of financial freedom, to really get your money matters in order, right? Wrong! You need to lay a firm foundation first.

A carpenter can know all about the mistakes he needs to avoid in constructing a house, but unless he avoids those mistakes while laying the foundation, his efforts may still produce a disaster.

There are four cornerstones you need to lay very carefully as a foundation for financial freedom in your life.

The first cornerstone is to *recognize that God owns everything*. Let's be clear about this basic principle. First, note what we are *not* saying. We are not saying you should *pretend* that God owns everything—you know these possessions are really yours but to have a good "spiritual" attitude you will say they all belong to God.

No, no, no. The Bible says that literally everything belongs to God. You may possess certain things, but you do not own them, for *possession is not ownership.*

When you say or think or assume that you have ownership rights, you place yourself in immediate conflict with God, for He claims those rights. "The earth is the Lord's, and the fulness thereof; the world, and they that dwell therein" (Ps. 24:1). Universal ownership—that's God's claim. And beyond saying that in a general way, He's also specific about it. "The silver is mine, and the gold is mine, saith the Lord of hosts" (Hag. 2:8). "For every beast of the forest is mine, and the cattle upon a thousand hills . . . and the wild beasts of the field are mine" (Ps. 50:10, 11).

So recognizing God as owner of all that we possess is not pious pretending that things are other than they are, but realizing the true facts.

Second, we are not saying that we should transfer ownership to God. Bill Gothard has helped many people with his seminars. In his Advanced Leadership Guide, he has a section on "Financial Freedom." I gladly acknowledge my indebtedness to Bill Gothard and to others in learning biblical principles relating to finances. However, Gothard says that we should "transfer ownership" of money, time, possessions, and earning power to God. This is an impossibility because we do not have ownership in the first place. You can't transfer title to something you don't own!

However, you can falsely claim ownership or you

can assume ownership of someone else's property, and that is precisely what I am warning against here (and what Gothard no doubt intends). God says everything is His, and our recognition of God's ownership is the first foundation stone of financial freedom.

How does God's ownership relate to my freedom? Well, for one thing, if God is the owner it relieves me of a certain amount of responsibility. I am still responsible to be a good manager of the property and resources He has put in my trust. But beyond that, I am free.

Before I became a Christian, I once ripped my trousers getting out of my car. In a rage I jumped back in, spun out of the parking lot (depositing about $3 worth of rubber), crossed two lanes of traffic, narrowly missing another car and generally causing my family great unpleasantness. All this over a pair of slacks!

By contrast, a year or so ago, I was walking through the kitchen when I snagged my suit pants, ripping them. As I looked down at them, my reaction was, "Oh, well, if that's what you want to happen to your pants." Then I found myself praising God for reminding me that I should slow down and watch what I was doing. I was getting a valuable lesson at a very inexpensive price (the slacks, by the way, were fixed at no cost by the cleaners and the repair is practically invisible.)

That is a rather mundane example; how about something more serious?

Suppose, for example, that I have an automobile accident through no fault of my own. I can say, "Okay, God, if that's what you want to allow to happen to your car, it's all right with me."

Really, I find it takes a lot of pressure off me when I recognize that all I have belongs to God.

I mean, if He wants some of His money to flow through me to the local auto repair shop, I'm willing. Or maybe it's His intention to supply me with another car about now, and He's allowed this to happen to get my attention. Or better yet, maybe I'm supposed to ride the bus to share Christ with another passenger.

Don't take this teaching too far and say that *God causes bad things* to happen. Remember that God is the source of everything good, while Satan stands in the wings looking to be a spoiler. I've known people to attribute very bad things to God: "He took our baby away to teach us a lesson." / "He burned our house down." / "He wiped us out financially." God did *not* do any of those things—Satan did; though, of course, God will bring good out of them as those involved trust Him.

As I have turned everything over to God, I've found that my possessions are in great hands. He's taken much better care of them than I was able to by myself.

So remember, *you possess, but God owns.*

In further establishing this cornerstone—recognizing God's ownership—you must realize that you do not earn your income independently. We can express it this way: *you earn, but God enables.*

The Bible warns against saying in your heart, "My power and the might of mine hand hath gotten me this wealth" (Deut. 8:17). Here's a fellow who says, "I am a self-made man. I did it. I pulled myself up by the bootstraps. I put myself through school. I started this business, and I made it a success."

God says, "No way!"

God says, "Thou shalt remember the Lord thy God: for it is he that giveth thee power to get wealth" (Deut. 8:18).

There is no such thing as a self-made man. There is only a man who refuses to recognize the power of God's hand in his life, because no one can make it financially without God.

You may think of some person who is not a Christian, who has never recognized God or given anything to God and yet is successful. But I say that person has nevertheless been enabled by God to earn anything and everything he has. For it is in God that we "live, and move, and have our being" (Acts 17:28).

Furthermore, people who are financially successful have become so by applying God's principles, perhaps without knowing it. Because if you don't apply the principles, you cannot be successful. The only exception is the person who gains his wealth dishonestly, and his success is the kind you can best do without.

You possess, but God owns.
You earn, but God enables.

The final step in recognizing that God owns everything is to realize that as Christians our commitment to God is not only "spiritual" but it relates to every aspect of our lives. In other words, if you have dedicated your life to Christ, *all you have is His also.*

Perhaps this concept is best expressed by the Apostle Paul when he writes, "I beseech ye therefore, brethren, by the mercies of God, that ye present your bodies a living sacrifice, holy, acceptable unto God, which is your reasonable service" (Rom. 12:1). To present our bodies a living sacrifice certainly means that all we are and have is dedicated to God. Our bodies include every member, so whether we work with our hands as laborers, with our mouths as speakers, with our feet as messengers, with our eyes as inspectors—with whatever member or combination of members—we are using bodies that belong to Christ.

And what does Paul say about this kind of complete dedication? It is your "reasonable service."

Such dedication is not "extreme fanaticism" but "reasonable service" on our part. Why reasonable? Because we belong to God by the virtue of the fact that He made us. "It is he that hath made us, and not we ourselves; we are his people, and the sheep of his pasture" (Ps. 100:3). Besides making us, He bought us with the precious blood of Christ. Don't you know that "ye are not your own? For ye are bought with a price: therefore glorify God in your body, and in your spirit, which are God's" (1 Cor. 6:19-20).

In view of God's double ownership of us, the only reasonable thing to do is to present ourselves to Him. And when we present ourselves, He owns all that we are and have.

You possess, but God owns.

You earn, but God enables.

You are God's, so all you have is God's.

Therefore recognize it: God owns everything.

3

Set Your Sights on Success

Once you have straightened out the question of ownership and have recognized God's absolute right to all you possess, you are in a position to set the next cornerstone—*to claim financial freedom.* Since you belong to God, and all that you possess belongs to God, in what condition do you suppose God wants His property (you and your goods) to be? Does He want His property all tied in knots over financial worries? Does He want His property to suffer neglect because of lack of adequate resources to care for it properly? Of course not.

God wants you to have financial freedom. But like every other special gift of God, financial freedom must be claimed by faith. "But let him ask in faith, nothing wavering. For he that wavereth is like a wave of the sea driven with the wind and tossed. For let not that man think that he shall receive any thing of the Lord" (James 1:6, 7).

Make a specific commitment to gain financial freedom. Then claim it, stick with your commitment, and it will be yours.

Remember, however, that God is not going to deliver you instantly. It took you perhaps five, ten, even twenty years or longer to get into the mess you are in. Give God a little time to work on you and get you out.

It's not that God cannot get you out of financial bondage instantly. He can. But would you learn—really learn—the lessons you need? Or would you soon be making some of the same old mistakes and getting yourself right back into trouble?

Here's the pattern. You begin to recognize that you have been doing things wrong, and you change your attitudes and actions. God slowly brings you out of your chaos as you apply the principles you learn.

Ultimately you gain complete freedom, and you *keep* it. You see, usually we have to learn our lessons one at a time, and not infrequently we have to relearn them several times before we really can be depended on to follow them.

This is true not only of finances but of all of life. We learn our lessons, and we seem to be going great guns, and then we blow it again. We look up dazedly to God from our prostrate position on the floor and we say, "God, what happened?" He reminds us of some principle we thought we had learned some time ago, and we say, "Oh, that one—I forgot about that. Sorry, Lord. But now I get your point, so will you please get me out of this mess?" And, of course, He gets you out. After a while you learn the lesson well enough to remember it.

So you need both patience and persistence. Be patient enough to allow God to work the necessary permanent changes in your life to enable you to have financial freedom. Be persistent in never losing sight of your goal. Never entertain the notion that you might not make it. Say, "Financial freedom will be mine," and press unflinchingly forward in that faith, for "what you say is what you get" (Mark 11:23 " . . . he shall have whatsoever he saith").

4

Seek the Right Goals

So far we have established that everything belongs to God and that He wants you to function in an atmosphere of financial freedom. But what is the grand design, the aim and object of this entire arrangement? In other words, *what do you intend to do with your material resources*? This brings us to the third cornerstone: *establish a spiritual purpose.*

I believe that the only valid spiritual purpose we as Christians can establish is to serve and honor Jesus Christ. More specifically, we should aim to present Jesus Christ and His way of life to others and then to lead to maturity those who receive Christ as their Savior and Lord.

This is, please note, a two-step process. We want to bring people to know Jesus Christ first of all. Then we have a real duty and obligation to share with them all the tremendous promises of God, all of the wonderful advantages that are theirs as Christians. For we are joint heirs with Christ.

What has all of this to do with finances? A great deal. It profoundly affects your attitude toward and use of your resources. Because if your spiritual purpose is to serve Christ as I have just described, all of your resources become ministering currency toward that end.

Our home is ministering currency. We have had nine foster teenagers in our home over the last six or seven years. Four of them are now Christians, three are "churchians," and two are still being claimed.

One girl who came to us had never been inside a church in her entire life and she was fifteen years old at the time. Her only concept of Jesus Christ was as a two-part swear word. She did not know He was an actual historical character, that He was God come in the flesh, that He died on the cross. She's a sister in Christ now and she's going to heaven because our home was open; it was ministering currency for the Lord.

Now, this wasn't easy. This particular girl had lived a very rough life. The only fun she had ever had was at night after her parents passed out drunk. She would sneak out of her house about midnight and be gone until 6 a.m., running the streets with a gang of kids. With a background like that, you know she still has problems. But she's beginning to change, and she's headed for heaven now.

Your home becomes ministering currency when you entertain God's people there. We have had four to eight couples staying with us at one time while they attended seminars or conferences in our area.

My telephone is ministering currency. If I'm with a teenager when he gives his life to Christ, I give him some great Bible verses to rely on—Romans 10:9, 10 or John 3:16 or 1 John 5:10-12—and then write my name and phone number in the flyleaf of his Bible. "Listen," I say, "if Satan ever hassles you and says, 'Hey, you're not a Christian, you couldn't be a Christian and act this way,' you call me collect any time you want to."

So they call. Maybe all they want is for someone to love them, to talk to them, to care about them. It may take me a few moments at 3 a.m. to realize who is calling, but that's all right. We always accept collect phone calls at our house; we never say no.

My clothes are ministering currency. I have about sixteen different styles of lapel "fish" pins. One day I found myself in an elevator with three stewardesses and two passengers heading toward our flight. One said, "What's that pin you're wearing?"

I always say the same thing. "That's my *ichthus* pin. That's Greek for fish, and it's the symbol the early Christians used to identify one another. But the interesting thing is that the individual characters in the word also have meaning. They stand for 'Jesus Christ—God's Son—Savior,' and this is the testimony of my life—that even though I don't deserve it, Jesus Christ, God's Son, is my Savior." And then I just smile.

You know, that's the Gospel—Jesus Christ, God's Son, Savior.

I have never had anyone on an elevator, a street corner, or in the store fall to his knees to receive Christ. But I am ministering the Gospel and I believe God will use my witness. Someone hearing about my pin may think, "What is that dummy talking about? I have been a Lutheran [or Catholic or Protestant or whatever] all my life." He may just dismiss me and my testimony. But when a crisis comes in his life, or when some other witness speaks to him, or when he sees Billy Graham on TV, God may use my witness along with that of others to speak to his heart.

I am not responsible for individuals accepting Christ; I am responsible for sharing the Gospel as I have opportunity. And when I use my material goods to witness, I have converted them into min-istering currency.

There are other ways too. Every community has rest homes and nursing homes occupied by elderly people whose hearts are just crying for someone to show them some love. Once a week you could take some of these people shopping or to the doctor or just out for a ride. Suddenly your car becomes min-istering currency.

We have a swimming pool, and it's ministering currency. You may as well know about our swim-ming pool right now. When we talk later about de-veloping sales resistance, figuring out what things actually are costing you, and so on, you may get the impression that we pinch every penny and can never have anything nice. Not so. It's just that you have to be realistic about what you can afford, and you have to spend with some intelligence and fore-sight, not just by impulse.

Before we ever bought our swimming pool, I had to consider all the overhead involved: water, filter, chlorine, chemicals, gas to heat the water, in-surance, cleaning costs, tools, decking, increased taxes (in my case no taxes because it's an above-ground pool), and a fence all around for safety lest some neighborhood child wander in.

How about extra cleaning costs in the house from water and dirt being tracked in? What about extra towels and swimming suits for people who come over unprepared and then want to go swimming? How about the extra soft drinks and snacks for our swim-ming pool guests? These are all extra costs that must be included because I wouldn't have a pool that was not ministering currency. That is God's pool, so all of God's children can come over and use it.

A couple of evenings last summer when the hour got late, we said, "Goodnight everybody. When you get done, be sure to close the door and turn out the lights." Then we went to bed and left them swimming. Why not? It's God's swimming pool. And our guests had complete freedom to go to our refrigerator and get something to eat. We want everything we possess to be ministering currency.

Get the picture?

Recognize God's ownership.

Claim financial freedom.

Establish a clear spiritual purpose.

That brings us to the fourth cornerstone of our foundation, *tithe your income,* which we will consider in the next chapter.

5

Save the Tithe from Satan

I began my life within the church about eleven years ago. Billy Graham was coming to town and my wife, who was very interested in spiritual things at that time, decided she wanted to be a counselor for the crusade. So we both went to the crusade counselor training sessions. We went through the whole series and qualified as counselors. Now, I was not a Christian at the time. But, you know, it was easy enough to memorize and be able to use four Bible references.

At that time I had an intellectual understanding of the "process" through which people became Christians. It all made sense to me, too, because some people were pretty wicked and they needed this. Personally, I already had it all together; I didn't need anything. I had a real good relationship with God: I didn't bother Him, and He didn't bother me.

Later at the crusade, when it came time for Dr. Graham to call the people to Christ and the counselors were going forward to pray with them, this one "qualified counselor" couldn't move. I just stayed rooted in place, and I didn't know why. Of course, I know now. Christ was not real to me, and there was no way I could share Him with anyone else. So I sat through the Graham Crusade not understanding that he was talking to me, that I needed to receive Christ as my Savior and Lord.

I started then to attend a small church in southwest Portland. I would show up about half the time, depending on who was playing on the Sunday morning TV football game. I began to enjoy going to church. The pastor made a good outline of everything he presented, and I would then go home and study it.

About this time my wife and I made a commitment to become tithers in the church we were attending. Remember, I was not even a Christian at this time. But if you are going to play the church game, you are supposed to tithe. Even people who are not Christians know that—which is one reason they stay away from church, so it won't cost them any money. But I figured if I was going to play the game, I'd play it right. I'd pay the monthly dues.

The next thing I knew we received notice from our landlord that he was selling the house we were renting and we had to move. We began looking for a place to rent and couldn't find one, except for some that were priced significantly higher than I thought they ought to be. We decided if we were going to spend that much money for housing, we'd buy. So we made an offer on a house, but it was refused. We made another offer and they turned that one down.

We finally decided to pray about it. "Lord, we really want this house," we prayed. "If you want us to have this house, we're going to have to take the money we had dedicated for your tithe and put it with the offering for the house. So we're going to make them that offer, and if that's okay with you, let it go through."

Then I made a side deal with the Lord. In our church they had a time when the pastor would open the service up for the Holy Spirit to do whatever He wanted. An individual might stand and lead in prayer, another individual might give a testimony, somebody else might lead out in a song. So I said, "Lord, if you honor this and we get the house, I will get up in the service Sunday morning and give a testimony on how you answer prayer." I figured God would really be impressed by that.

I proceeded to work out one of the most beautiful "spontaneous" three-minute, four-point prayer outlines you ever heard. It was a good sermon. I was all ready to give it on Sunday morning, because, as a matter of fact, the offer was accepted. So, guess what? They had an evangelist in and he didn't have a sharing time. He just got up and started preaching.

The next thing I knew he had us all standing and was talking about the need for some of us to come down and kneel at that altar and to accept Christ as Savior. There could just as well have been a neon sign flashing up there—"MacGregor, this is your turn to receive Christ."

I needed to go, and I did. It was November 10, 1968, a little bit after 12 noon when I received Christ as my Savior.

Just to finish that story, three months later the Lord increased my salary by $275 a month. I began tithing a full 10% and I have been tithing ever since. In fact, we give substantially more than 10% of our income.

At that time, being an accountant, I dedicated myself to learning and understanding what the Bible has to say about finances.

You know, the Bible is a remarkable Book. If you were to be a great leader, it seems to me you would want to go to the world's great leaders and ask them what it takes. What are the elements of good leadership? One of the greatest leaders the world has ever seen was Moses, a man who led an entire nation through a searing ordeal. You can go to Moses for advice because the secrets of his leadership are revealed in the Bible.

If you want to be wealthy, you would go to the wealthiest men in the world and ask what they did to acquire and manage this wealth. What principles did they follow? The wealthiest man the world has ever seen was Solomon, and his principles are set forth in the Bible. You see, the Bible has all the answers we need in order to handle our finances properly.

One interesting discovery I made concerns tithing. Some Christians seem to feel that tithing—giving 10% of one's income—is a legalist hang-up. It is of the law. Christ has delivered them from the law, so they don't have to tithe. They operate by the verse that says to give as God has prospered us (1 Cor. 16:2). Some Christians feel that God hasn't done such a good job of prospering them so they are prospering Him in the same way—very little.

The fact is that tithing is valid for Christians. It is a valid biblical principle apart from the law. As a matter of fact, God considers tithing so important that He established it as a principle before the law was ever given. Genesis 14 contains the first mention of tithing in the Bible. Abraham, the father of the Jewish nation, was coming back from battle bringing the spoils of war, a fabulous treasure he had captured. Melchizedek, the king of Salem, came out to meet him, and we read that Abraham "gave him tithes of all" (Gen. 14:20).

Now, this Melchizedek is a very mysterious and interesting individual. Some Bible scholars believe that he was really Christ himself in a preincarnate appearance. I think the biblical evidence supports that view. In any case, the record states that Melchizedek was "the priest of the most high God" (Gen. 14:18), and Abraham paid him tithes. This was some 400 years before the law was given through Moses. I find it interesting that the tithe concept was taught to Abraham, a man of faith, not to Moses, a man of law.

Somebody says, "Okay, so tithing was practiced before the law was given, but Christ never taught it; it's not in your New Testament."

Oh? Read Matthew 23:23: "Woe unto you, scribes and Pharisees, hypocrites! for ye pay tithe of mint and anise and cummin, and have omitted the weightier matters of the law—judgment, mercy, and faith: these ought ye to have done, and not to leave the other undone." Notice that last phrase about not leaving the other undone. What "other"? The paying of tithes.

Jesus is saying that of course you ought to tithe. Anybody knows you are supposed to tithe, but don't get bogged down in the legalism of tithing and imagine that nothing more is required. Go on beyond the tithe and get involved with individuals in the areas of wisdom, truth, justice—really share with people. This you ought to do, but don't leave the other (the tithing) undone.

For that matter, the New Testament principle of giving "as God has prospered" doesn't contradict tithing. If God has prospered you with $10,000, you ought to give $1000. If He has provided you with only $1000, your tithe would be $100. Isn't that giving "as God has prospered"?

We are stewards, we don't own anything. God gives us money to manage. Now, we can do anything we want with that money. But let me tell you, one of two things is going to happen with the tithe—it will either be given to God or it will be collected by Satan.

People ask, "What do you mean 'it will be collected by Satan'?" I mean it will go for things that have absolutely no lasting value. I can see this in my own past life, and I have seen it in the lives of many people with whom I have counseled. The unpaid tithe may go toward keeping up with the next door neighbors: they get a new car, and you don't really need one, but you can't be driving around in the old one, so you extend beyond your means just to buy a new car. Maybe it will go for flashy clothes, for unexpected bills, medical payments, accidental losses—any number of things. Wherever it goes, you will never have anything of lasting value from it. You won't be able to point to a house, you won't be able to point to a boat, you won't be able to point to anything and say, "That's where my tithe went." No, it's just gone.

As a CPA, when I do a cash audit, I pin down exactly how every penny came and where it went. I create what is called a Source and Application Funds Statement, showing exactly where all the money came from and what it was spent for and where. I have had opportunity with several couples to do exactly this, to go through their budgets and show how God has honored their tithing.

One couple attended a church that had annual pledges, and they pledged $5 a week. Things were rough; they could hardly pay their bills, so the next year they cut their pledge to $2.50 a week. Their situation got even worse. They finally got to the point where they were not giving anything and they were paying a tiny amount monthly, as little as one dollar each on a whole raft of little bills—doctor bills, dentist bills, car repair bills, and so on.

At last this couple decided to start over again by faith and begin tithing. Remember, nothing had been going right for them. But after four months of tithing, every one of those doctor, dentist, and repair bills had been paid. They were eating better than ever before in their lives, and they had $82 in savings.

I thought, *Here is one situation where I can really get in and analyze exactly how the money came in and where it went.* I discovered that during the time when they started tithing, he did not get a raise, he did not have a bonus, she did not go to work, no extra money came in, and nobody wrote off any bills. I proved beyond a shadow of a doubt that there was absolutely no earthly way for them to have tithed their income, paid all those bills, saved $82, and eaten as well as they did. And I would stake my professional reputation on it—it was an impossibility. But they did it!

When God is involved in one's finances, the rules of the professionals don't always fit. I have done similar studies with four separate couples and in every case all I proved is that what they did "cannot be done."

If you bring your tithe into the storehouse, if you take 10% right off the top whether you can afford it or not, God guarantees to meet your needs, and your family will never suffer anything for the lack of that money.

Fantastic things happen when people obey God's

prompting to give. One time Meg and I wanted to meet a need presented in a special appeal at church. It required $150 and we didn't have it to spare. We prayed about it; we didn't rush into it. We really sought the Lord and concluded that we ought to give our food money for the month of November to this need. "Okay, Lord, that means the Mac-Gregors eat this month on you or they don't eat at all," I reminded Him.

We gave the $150 on a Sunday, and by the next Friday nothing special had happened. Our food supply was getting lower, and there was no money to replenish it. I was scheduled to go to Idaho for a Sunday morning, afternoon, and evening series on giving and money management. So Friday morning I was in prayer, and I said, "Now listen, God, this is me, remember? You said that if we asked and believed, you would supply our needs. Now we have some needs here, Lord. We are going to Idaho and I don't even have gas for the round trip; there is no food, there's no money for anything. I am planning to tell those people in Idaho that they need to tithe to be able to receive your blessing. But if you don't meet my needs, I'll have to tell on you."

Does that sound brash? Well, suppose I came to you on a Sunday and said, "Look, don't worry about going out and buying groceries this coming week because I am going to bring over three bags full."

"Fine," you reply, "praise the Lord."

Friday morning comes, and I haven't showed up. You pick up the phone and say, "Are you going to bring the groceries? No hassle if you don't but you did say you would."

That's what I told God: "No hassle, but you said

you would. How can I go over and tell these people that you always meet needs if you are not meeting mine?"

That afternoon I phoned home and Meg said, "God sent us $25 in the mail."

It was from a tax return I had done in April, and here it was November. I had talked with that man just three weeks before. He had been in an automobile accident two months previously, and had been out of work that whole time, receiving no income. He was also going through a divorce, was three months behind on his child support to his first wife, and had not paid his taxes from the prior April, for which IRS was threatening to foreclose on him. Now here was his check for $25 and a little note saying, "I don't know why but I felt I just had to send it to you."

I knew why. I hadn't needed it in April and I was not going to need it in December, but I surely needed it in November and that's when God provided it.

So we left for Idaho. Now, this particular church we ministered in was not known for outstanding giving. Though this was my third visit there, it was the first time they gave me a love offering—$48.

Later at home Meg picked up a book that she had been reading; there was a $10 check as a bookmark. (Quite an expensive bookmark!)

At Thanksgiving we had twenty-three people coming over for dinner; yet we had no turkey and no money for the trimmings. Then the phone started ringing. Someone had gotten a good deal on rolls and was bringing enough for the dinner. Somebody else was bringing the salad. Several guests were bringing other things. The only food we had to buy was the turkey, and we found some on sale for 29 cents a pound. We had just enough money to get a twenty-two-pound turkey.

That's the way it went—coincidence followed coincidence the whole month long. Why, we ate so well that month I was tempted to try it again in December. Fantastic!

I shared this at an 8 a.m. service in Eugene. One couple in financial straits got so excited about tithing that they went home and collected every penny they had in the house. They broke open piggy banks and went through all their drawers, finding every cent they had and putting it in a bag. Then they came back to the 11 a.m. service carrying this big heavy bag of coins.

These people were not going to be paid again until a week from the next Monday—eight days. They had a quarter tank of gas in their pickup truck and their food supply was low, but they wanted to do this to show God they were serious about tithing and trusting Him to provide for them.

Of course, the first thing Satan did was to hassle me with doubts. What if they should give up about Wednesday and decide God was not going to meet their needs? But I said, "No, Satan, get out of here." We went to prayer right there and claimed God's promise for them.

We had counted the money and found $17.10 in the coin bag. The next morning that woman opened her purse and was startled to see a $20 bill. She has a very simple explanation—God materialized that $20 bill in her purse.

I'm not going to argue. I don't know how it happened; all I know is that the money was not there on Sunday and when they needed it on Monday, it was there. God provides.

If we step out on faith and keep trusting, God will

meet our needs no matter how far behind our bills are.

I believe there is no way in Scripture to support bankruptcy; it's not a viable alternative for Christians. To take bankruptcy is to say, "My God is not so great after all, because I got myself into this mess and He can't get me out of it. I'm going to have to go through a legal action to get myself out of this." It's a puny God who can't take care of a problem like that.

I remember, though, a time when I came as close as I ever have in my life to saying, "Have you thought about bankruptcy?" I tell you, this man was in trouble. He didn't own his own home, his car or anything else. He had a total of $800 in assets and $27,000 worth of debts, some of which were pressing him like crazy.

I said, "Look, you're going nowhere anyway, right? So why don't you give God a chance?" He had heard me talk about giving the tithe and even above the tithe, expecting God to bless it and multiply it back, so he gave $120.

The next morning he got a telephone call: "I'd like you to come over and make a bid on a job. If it's $25,000 or under, you've got it." (He had heard about and seen my friend's work and liked it.)

"I'd love the job and I need it desperately," my friend replied, "but I've got nothing. I had to lay off my crew, I owe $27,000, and nobody in this town will extend me any credit. There's no way I can take the job."

The man said, "I'll advance you $8,000 to pay your crew, and you can have the suppliers bill me for materials as you go along."

The next day he got a similar phone call from someone else. Within three weeks he had so much business that he was praying that God would stop blessing him. Why? Because he stepped out on faith, even though his logical mind told him it was stupid to give $120 away when he owed $27,000.

You know, when I get down to the end of a month and I'm $20 short of being able to meet my bills, I give God another $30 and say, "Okay, God, I'm $50 short. Now it's your responsibility." And God provides. He just brings in the money, enabling me to take care of the bills. How? Maybe it's extra money I'm not expecting, or I may think I have to have something done on the car for $120 and it turns out to be $40. He works in any number of ways.

Tithing always works when we are faithful. God blesses us, and our families never suffer. I am so convinced this is true that during seminars I make this promise: *If you are not tithing now, start with your next paycheck. Take 10% of your gross wage right off the top and continue doing that for three months. If at the end of three months, God has not met your needs and you have bills that are unpaid strictly because of the amount of money you are tithing, send me the bills and I'll pay them.* I can afford it so I don't worry about it. It won't hurt me. I must tell you that since making this promise in 1972, I've never yet paid such a bill. God is faithful.

Now, I am not saying that if you tithe, you're going to get out of debt at once. As a matter of fact, just the opposite may seem to be true. You see, if you're not tithing, then Satan has been getting that money and using it for his kingdom. When Satan sees you giving the tithe where it belongs, he'll be upset and throw everything he can at you. Satan has no patience, however, and I've never seen him last the three months. You stick to your tithe commitment and God *guarantees* to bless.

Several years ago I held a seminar in Medford, Oregon. The night before the seminar, one young couple sat down and totaled their debts—over $4,000. Of this amount, $1,800 was due Monday or wages were going to be garnished, a car repossessed, and he would lose his job. Things looked bleak.

After the seminar, they made a commitment to begin tithing and, very importantly, to get out of debt and stay out. Later that year I returned to Medford and this couple shared with me that three months to the day marked the payoff of all the $4,000 in debts. In reviewing their cash flow for the three months, they were unable to account for $1,900 and felt I might be able to help. Having suffered the frustration of trying to reconcile God's accounting system, I declined!

Another couple that had attended the same seminar also shared this with me. Their story is more typical of what I see God doing after a tithe commitment. Three months after their commitment, they almost sent me $450 in bills (his salary was $1500 a month). In praying about it, he said he found himself saying, "Well, we're no worse off three months later than we were before we began tithing. Everybody's eating, we have clothes, we're no further behind in bills than we were." He decided to continue tithing to see what would happen.

Several months later they figured out that with two more years of very carefully sticking to their budget and watching their pennies, they would be out of debt.

What a drag! Right?

This is why I have emphasized, as one of the foundations of financial freedom, committing yourself to getting out of debt. It takes time. What this

couple said next, however, is extremely important!
"As we look at the two years ahead of us, our minds
say, 'Wow, we're giving away $150 a month! If we
used this money to retire debts, doubling up on payments, we'd be out of debt and able to minister in
total freedom.' We won't do that, however, because
we know if God does not get that money, Satan will
collect it. We won't be any better off, no debts will
be retired sooner, and, in fact, we will never be debt-
free as long as God is not getting His tithe."

How well this couple understands God's perfect
plan. To see it illustrated, consider Joshua's conquest
of Jericho.

Remember that when Abraham returned from a
victory with all the spoils, he gave a tithe to the
priest of God. But in the case of Jericho, God said,
"And the city shall be accursed, even it, and all
that are therein, to the Lord" (Josh. 6:17).

What is this? God is claiming all of Jericho!
Why? The key is found in the word "accursed."
The Hebrew for this word is *cherem*—devoted to
destruction. Whenever such a curse was pronounced
on a city, it meant that *everything in it* was to be
completely burned in fire or consecrated at the altar
of God.

It is interesting to note that the Lord specified
a penalty for taking of the accursed thing, not only
to the person taking, but to the whole nation (v.
18). In terms of our day, this means that when you
withhold the tithe, you hurt not only yourself, but
also your entire church. How so?

Joshua 7 describes the sending of a small con-
tingent of 3,000 warriors to take the small town of
Ai. To have sent the whole army would be about
the same as directing the total military might of
the United States against Haiti. This should have

been a sure victory. Yet they had thirty-six of their men killed and were repulsed in utter defeat.

Joshua followed the custom of all prophets of God: cast himself into the dirt and began throwing dust over his head. God tells Joshua to get up. "You blew it; you took of the accursed thing, you stole from Me. Now I've turned My back on you until you destroy the accursed thing from among you" (see vv. 11, 12).

Achan is finally identified as the culprit. He took a Babylonian robe, 200 shekels of silver and 50 shekels of gold—a total value of about $2500. Joshua then had Achan and his entire household stoned to death and burned with fire.

This seems to be a harsh penalty for a minor offense, but remember that God said that Jericho was accursed (*cherem*) and anyone who took of the accursed thing would suffer the penalty of being utterly destroyed.

What is the principle? Simply this: God had promised the children of Israel ten cities; Jericho was the first. It was the first tenth of God's increase, and the first tenth of *anything* in God's economy is *cherem*—devoted to destruction!

The first tenth of your income is *cherem*. Now, you don't have to give it to God, but if you don't, it will be devoured by Satan. You will not improve your standard of living, acquire extra assets, or get out of debt sooner. *It will be destroyed.*

That's why I can make the promise to underwrite the tithe. There is no way for me to have to pay because if God is not getting the tithe, Satan is. When you step out in faith and begin to tithe, you place yourself in the position where God can do for you what He promised to Israel, "pour you out a blessing, that there shall not be room enough to receive it" (Mal. 3:10).

Tithing works—and it's a critical element in successful Christian money management.

Build your financial planning on a firm foundation: recognize God's ownership, claim financial freedom, establish a clear spiritual purpose, and tithe your income.

Afterthought

We are still making this promise and as of October 1987 still haven't paid anything. I want to honestly share with you that we have been tested several times. Most often, it is a situation where someone feels hurt and abandoned by God. With prayer and counsel, we've been able to boost every challenger to victory!

PART III

Learning Practical Money Management

6

How To Know a Good Buy
When You See It

Let me share with you a little rule that has saved my wife and me hundreds, even thousands, of dollars. By following our "delayed action" rule, we have saved money on encyclopedias, dishes, dishwashers, sets of great books, china, a fire-alarm system—you name it.

The rule is this: When the salesman is all done making his pitch, we say, "Thank you, we will let you know within a day or so what our decision is." If a salesman has come to our home, we ask him to call us back in the morning. If we have gone shopping for a car or an appliance or other major purchase, we say, "We will come back in a couple of hours and let you know what we have decided."

One reason for doing this is so husband and wife can talk the matter over alone. This is how such a conversation has gone for us several times:

"Well, Hon, we want it; why don't we go ahead and get it?"

"Okay, if you really want it."

"If *I* want it!? I thought *you* wanted it."

"Well, I don't especially want it."

"That settles it; we won't get it."

A second reason for the "delayed action" rule is to give you a chance to coolly evaluate the purchase without the pressure of the sales pitch unduly influencing you. You should have a chance to get away and ask, "Do we need this right now? Is this the place and way to purchase it?"

I know it is not easy to tell some salesmen to wait. I've been through it. Scene: The MacGregor home. Time: Almost 10 p.m. Situation: We've had the salesman's pitch and he's trying to sign us on the dotted line. "Would you please leave," I say, "and we will call you tomorrow."

"Well, really, Mr. and Mrs. MacGregor, you know at the very beginning I showed you on the chart how it costs $75,000 a minute to advertise on a program like 'The Waltons,' and how market surveys show that after six and a half months of advertising—over a $3,000,000 budget—we developed absolutely no product identification with the people we wanted to reach. So we decided to take that advertising budget and pass it along to you in the way of reduced costs. And you said at the very beginning that you liked that idea and would be a very active promoter of a fine product marketed that way, did you not?"

"Yes, that's what we said."

"Well, now, if there is any hesitation on your part, Mr. and Mrs. MacGregor, if you cannot enthusiastically endorse this product, if you can't immediately say, 'Yes, this is something that I want to have in my home and to show my friends,' then you will not be the kind of advertiser that my sales manager says we must have. And so I am afraid that we cannot come back. We are required to make this presentation only once, and if there is any hesitation we just cannot come back. You must make up your mind tonight."

That is "close" number one. Don't buy it. Stick with your delayed action rule regardless.

I've been a salesman and I know some of the tricks. I "gave away" encyclopedias for a summer. I got a $90 commission on those "free" encyclopedias, my sales manager got about a $15 commission, his manager got about $10, the area manager got another $10, and I don't know what the regional manager got. By the time you were done, those free books cost you $400, most of it probably going for commissions.

Of course, you didn't pay anything for the encyclopedias, but you signed for the yearbook at $10 a year for ten years and the question-answering service at $30 a year for ten years.

Did you ever send a question to one of those encyclopedia places? Most people don't. I have sent in three and got three very poor answers. (Someone who heard me mention this in a seminar differed with me; he used the service and got an A+ on a term paper!)

My whole point is that we need to make our purchasing decisions away from the pressure of the sales pitch.

A salesman came out to sell us a home fire-alarm system. I don't want to knock the product, but the sales pitch was based on fear. When that salesman got through, to delay buying his fire-alarm system seemed equivalent to saying, "Well, the kids haven't really excited us that much anyway, so if they burn to death tonight...!" But we stuck to our rule through close number 1, 2, and 3 and he finally left.

To Buy or Not To Buy

It's still necessary, of course, to make the decision whether or not to buy. So, talk it over as husband and wife. Then the next step I highly recommend is to seek counsel. One important source of advice is your parents. I would not make a major decision in my life without first seeking the counsel of my parents and my wife's parents.

My dad has bought ten cars. If I am going to buy a car, why should I not consult him? I could learn a few things.

Meg's mom suggested something on the fire-alarm system that I hadn't even considered. Why not check the stores and compare costs?

Anything sold door-to-door usually costs you more, so compare the product and the price at the store. Also check mail order houses. We discovered that we could buy a comparable fire-alarm system for about $120. What had the salesman's price been? Between $500 and $600.

I am going to list eleven questions to ask yourself when considering a purchase in order to avoid impulse buying. You don't ask these questions about everything you buy, such as, 'Let's see, should I buy this head of lettuce?' You would never get through your grocery list! Set a dollar figure, perhaps $50. Anytime you are going to spend more than $50 on anything, ask these questions.

Do I really need it? You need to be especially careful about this when you go to garage sales and when you encounter unexpected "blue light" bargains in the stores. I was in a store when they announced a super-special: regular $1.98 for $.09. I dashed over and bought four boxes of tiles, four tiles in each box, and on each tile was a cartoon character: Huey Duck, Speedy Gonzalez, etc. So here I am taking home four boxes of tile, and I don't have the slightest idea what to do with them. "Here, Hon, look at this good deal I got!"

Okay, that's no big loss, and we said the checklist

was for items over $50. But there's no point buying *anything* you don't need, even if it only costs 36¢. For items over $50, the question is just that much more important. A man is walking through the store and notices a beautiful stereo sitting there. It happens to be playing and he likes it. *Hmm, I have been thinking about buying a stereo for a couple of years,* he thinks. (Actually he has thought about it very little and has not checked out the product and price at all.) *It surely would be nice, and the tag says it's on special.* So he buys it. The next week he finds out his kid sister has one to practically give away because she's getting married and her fiance already has one.

Is the price reasonable? Along with this, ask another question: *Is this the best time of year to buy?* The time to get the lowest price on a new car is in the fall. You will never get a better price because the new models have arrived and the prior year models will just sit on the floor unless they are discounted. So you *can* get a significant savings if you bargain for it.

But then there is another question: *If it is a bargain price, is it a current model?* The answer in the case of the car obviously is no. What difference does that make? You are going to be driving a car that is already one year old according to the Blue Book. In just a few months it will be almost two years old. And the resale price or trade-in value is going to reflect that. You will get an extra $100 to $300 for it being low mileage, but its worth is going to be reduced much more than that because of its year model. Unless you keep that new car at least six years—until depreciation ceases to be a major factor—your bargain may prove to be an unwise purchase. A new car depreciates 1/3 in the first year and an additional 20% in the second year.

For the best prices by all means shop for special sales, but be careful. *If the item is on sale, is it a true sale price?* You often read advertising like "40% off our regular price." But what *is* their regular price? Is it reasonable or inflated? You simply have to do comparison shopping.

Often discount stores will get in a large shipment of merchandise. You can tell the items are going to be "on sale" because they are stacked at the end of the aisle and marked, say, $14.97. Don't buy now. If you have shopped around, you will probably have found that these are selling for $12.98. Now comes the big sale, "Regular $14.97—now $10.98." Okay, it's not a $4 savings as you are supposed to think, but it is a $2 savings. So maybe you should buy, or wait for a sale at a place selling them for $12.98; they might be marked down to $7.98.

Many shoppers erroneously assume that whatever has a special tag on it is on sale. Not so. Observe what the tag actually says. Some will say "Featured Today." That may not mean a thing. But people who don't check prices will buy it. Another favorite is "Special Purchase." This label often identifies inferior merchandise bought by the store at low prices and sold the same way. So be aware of these words used to market merchandise and check which ones offer genuine savings.

Have you ever heard of a store *increasing* the price of its sale items? I can assure you it happens. No merchant would be foolish enough to attempt to get away with this all the time, but many stores do it now and then.

A leading department store got in a large shipment of umbrellas, and I liked them. I needed an umbrella, but the price was $7.50, and I thought that was a little high, so I waited. They had too many of them, so I felt sure they would be put on sale. I checked back each time I was in the store and finally my patience was rewarded. There were the umbrellas in the middle of the aisle with the store's special sale tag on them. Ah ha! A second look told me that they had been marked up to $9.50! (The store sold them all, too, but there was one customer they didn't catch!)

We buy tomato sauce often and were paying 33¢ for two cans. Then the same store ran a huge advertised special—6 cans for $1. Some savings! (Six cans at regular price would have been 99¢, right?)

Can I substitute something else for this? One of the best ways to save money is to substitute used for new. Buy a brand-new car today and it will probably drop $2,000 in value the first year. A friend of mine bought a new car because he got a fleet discount through his employer. He purchased a $6,500* car for only $5,300. Less than a year later, tired of getting only nine miles per gallon, he checked its trade-in value. He was offered $2,600 for the gas-guzzler.

If you want to pay a high price to drive a brand-new toy for a few months, go ahead. I will never buy a new car again myself, even if I can buy it at fleet discount. I'll let somebody else take that loss.

Why buy brand-new appliances? Friends of ours got a Maytag washer/dryer combination just two years old, coppertone color, for $75. The seller had moved to a new house and wanted her appliances in avocado, so she went out and bought new appliances. And I want to tell you, our friends did not just get a washer. This Maytag was the super deluxe, three rinses, two washes, plays "Stars and Stripes Forever," and practically scratches your back. Why buy the cheapest, stripped-down new set for hundreds

*How do you like those 1975 figures? Hertz tells us a new car depreciates 33% of the sticker price the first year, 20% the second and 20% the third.

when you can have a deluxe set for $75?

Does this product have any major disadvantages? You may be buying an air-conditioner. It seems great, it really pours out the cold air. Wait! Is that thing going to make so much noise you can't converse in the daytime or sleep at night? Now, that's a major disadvantage! Try to find out if there are any disadvantages. One way to do this is to check the reports of consumer magazines (more on this later). Another way is to talk to people who already own the product.

Though excessive in price, will it satisfy an inner need? That's valid. God not only meets our absolute physical need but pleases to give us the desires of our hearts (see Ps. 37:4). You know, I have a few things on my desire list. Right at the top of my list is some beach property. I want a place right on the ocean with a beautiful view of the waves rolling in. Now, I do not need a place at the beach, but I want one and I'll receive it anytime the Lord wants to give it to me.

I have good credit and a good income. I could cruise up and down the coast looking for somebody willing to sell on a short-term contract with a minimum down payment and a balloon payment at the end, at which time I'd have to refinance, and so on. There is little doubt that I could get into a place down there almost any time. But when God is ready for me to have my place down at the beach, He will give it to me. It will come, because He says not only will He meet my needs but He will give me the desires of my heart. However, before He gives me a beach place, He is going to make sure that there are no problems—that it will not get in the way of my relationship with God or my family's relationship with God.*

---

*October 29, 1987—we just opened the mail and learned that our offer on our beach home was accepted—we move in December!

Have I checked and researched the item? People so often buy things on the spur of the moment without ever bothering to investigate it. There are good magazines such as *Changing Times* and *Consumer Report* which go to great lengths to evaluate various products. You don't even have to subscribe to the magazines. You can go to the library and get vast information on washing machines, dryers, cars, homes, appliances—virtually any major consumer product. You can learn exactly what the features are, what the disadvantages are, and how the product performed under thorough testing.

Organizations and businesses often employ a buyer, a highly paid individual who may spend weeks investigating various suppliers to come up with the best buy on a tractor, a truck, a car, a telephone system or whatever it happens to be. That institution knows that it is worth hiring someone to assure maximum utilization of their dollars spent. You must do the same thing—check and research these items. This procedure is a great protection against impulse buying. You say, "I really want it, but I haven't checked into it yet; so I'll buy it after I have done a little research."

Do I know the retailer's reputation? A phone call to your local Better Business Bureau wouldn't hurt. MacGregor's rule? Always deal with a Christian brother or sister if possible.

Does the retailer offer any special services? This is a good question to ask when you are doing comparison shopping. For instance, you are going to buy a rug. One retailer just installs a rug and the other one installs a rug and cleans it free twice during the first year for the same price. Go with the second one. You may as well get some extra services with that purchase.

It is not necessary to have a yes answer to every one of the eleven questions. If you have nine to eleven yeses—buy; six to eight yeses—think carefully; zero to five yeses—don't buy.

Perhaps you have the impression that with all my financial know-how, I must really have it made. I don't. Although I have a good income and the Lord takes great care of us, I still blow it. But, you know, the times I get into financial trouble is when I think I am above the principles that I'm sharing. I think, "Look, I'm a CPA, and I understand cash flows, and I have good credit, so I will just go ahead and do it this way, because I can take care of the situation." And it never works out. I always get into trouble.

Anytime you violate these principles, you are going to be in trouble. Anytime you just go out and buy on impulse, it will probably turn out to be disastrous. Even if you can afford it, it may not be the best buy, or the best product, or even something you will use. And whether or not the mistake hurts you financially, you haven't been a good steward of the Lord's money.

7

How To Eat Well
Without Owning a Grocery Store

One evening when I came home from work, Meg said, "Honey, let's hop in the car and run down to the store real quick and get some meat. I've got everything else we need for dinner." So away we went, shopping for groceries on empty stomachs.

What was the very first thing we saw in the store? A great big display of Nabisco crackers: Wheat Thins, Hi Hos, Bacon Thins, everything but Triscuits; they are never on sale. (I am going to write Nabisco and ask them about that; it is appalling to Triscuit lovers.) This was some years ago, and these various crackers were on special for 37¢* a box, which was a super bargain. Naturally we bought a couple of boxes.

What was displayed right next to the crackers? Cheese, of course, and on the other side, bread-and-butter pickles. So along with our bargain crackers we picked up some pickles and some cheese at regular prices.

We couldn't have crackers, pickles, and cheese without salami; it just isn't done. So we went to the

*Were they ever that cheap? Multiply this by 3 plus for today's sale price. By the way, they now have Triscuit coupons!

back of the store for some Gallo dry salami. Not wanting to have only one kind of meat, we went over to the Oscar Mayer display and picked up some of their specialty meats. We didn't want to spend a lot of money, so we got the small packages that provide about four slices for 78¢.

Now it's obvious that we couldn't eat all those things without soft drinks, so we loaded some Coke and 7-Up into the basket. When you're facing the soft drinks, what is behind you? Potato chips, Fritos, and similar snack foods. We got a couple of boxes of potato chips—the ruffles type. You can't have dip chips without the dip, so we picked up one carton of clam dip and another with bacon and horseradish. (We always get two because I prefer one flavor and Meg wants another.) Going back down the aisle, we passed the frozen foods section. Look, a brand new item: frozen pizza rolls. That sounded so good we got a frozen pizza roll. Now we were all done. We checked out $14 worth of junk and headed for home. One thing we didn't buy. Did you notice what it was? We bought no meat for dinner.

Have you ever had a similar experience? You go on a shopping spree, you stuff your cart, and end up feeling terrible because you have bought more than anybody should, you're going to blow your diet and ruin your food budget. And, even worse, you know you are going to end up throwing some of this stuff away because you bought more than you can eat.

My unhappy story illustrates the importance of rule No. 1 for grocery shopping: *Never go to the store hungry.* I remember one time Meg sent me to the store for a couple of quarts of milk, and I came home with two huge bags of groceries—and no milk.

Maybe you have iron self-control. You are confronted with that tempting array of foodstuffs and remain unmoved. If so, congratulations; you are a rare specimen of an endangered species. The rest of us—the watering-mouth majority—cannot properly pray, "Lead us not into temptation" and then go to the grocery store hungry.

Rule No. 2: *Shop only once a week.* One of the real problems in wise grocery shopping is coping with the sophistication of the American marketing system. Marketing experts have spent millions of dollars studying you to learn what makes you buy. Your favorite supermarket is designed accordingly so that you will buy at the maximum clip.

If a product is displayed on the end of an aisle, people have a tendency to buy it, thinking it is on sale. Next time you're in a store, check this out and you'll find that less than half of these end-aisle displays actually contain sale merchandise.

On about 72% of your shopping trips you will pick up either meat or dairy products. Merchants recognize this so they make it easy on you by putting these things up front where they are easy to get. Right? Wrong! The meat and dairy cases are at the back of the store or at opposite ends so you will have to walk past many other tempting items to pick up what you came for.

A study of store layouts reveals several other interesting facts. The sketch on the next page is typical of floor arrangements you will find in stores throughout the country. Several things will almost always be true. If the store has a fresh bakery, it will be next to the produce section. This is because most customers start their shopping with the fresh produce. Since many bakery products are impulse items, the merchants want to get you early in your trip with good smelling things. If the bakery is not next to the fresh produce, it will be inside the right-hand door, because most shoppers are right-handed and tend to enter the right-hand door.

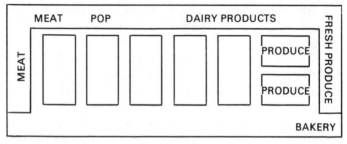

Note that there are an odd number of aisles. This means if you go up one aisle and down the next, you will end up at the back of the store and have to pass by one more aisle of merchandise before you get out.

What this all boils down to is that the store is laid out to get you to buy as much as possible, so you want to expose yourself to this tempting array as few times as possible. Shop only once a week.

Rule No. 3: *When you shop, use a list.* I heard on a special news broadcast one time that less than 5% of all grocery shoppers actually use a list and stick to it. You may use a list that says meat, cheese, eggs, cereal, salt, and flour, but then you leave the store with $43 worth of groceries. When I say you should use a list, I mean you should have a complete list of items you need from the store and stick exclusively to it. This will enable you to go through this marketing man's paradise without being seduced by the vast array of goodies you didn't plan to buy and truly don't need.

Many women tell me that planning their meals for one or two weeks at a time dictates the shopping list for them. The objective of all this is to have planned spending, which will naturally result in less spending.

Rule No. 4: *Take advantage of coupon offers.* Notice the order here. Don't let your coupons dictate what you will buy, but decide what you are going to buy and then go to your coupons. We receive over $600 worth of coupons a year in the Portland metropolitan area through the mail and magazines and newspapers.

Dial soap had a promotion: send in five Dial soap wrappers and they would refund you $1. I found four bars of Dial soap on sale for 88¢ so I bought a fifth one for another 22¢. My total cost was $1.10, plus 10¢ for a stamp. That's $1.20 into the purchase, and they sent me back a dollar. So it actually cost me 20¢ for five bars of Dial soap. Is that so much effort to mail in the wrappers?

I drink Sanka coffee. Once I sent in four of those little envelopes that cost 15¢ in the store, and they sent me back $2 and refunded my postage besides.

A word of caution on mailer coupon offers, though. Don't neglect to mail them in. Some people see the promotion in the store, think what a good deal it is, buy, and then never get around to sending for their refund. To avoid this, do it just as soon as you get home and unpack your shopping bag.

Use your "cents-off" coupons when you make purchases. On one $45 grocery bill, we used $4 worth of coupons—a 9% savings.*

Rule No. 5: *Shop alone.* If you take somebody else with you, it is going to cost you more.

Advertisers spend thousands of dollars pitching products such as breakfast cereals to children. They practically buy out Saturday morning TV programming for this purpose. Why? Because they know, even if you don't, that children can influence the purchasing habits of their parents. So when you go shopping leave the children—and Tony the Tiger—home.

Rule No. 6: *Check the lower shelves.* Here we are

---

*Did you see the Coupon Lady on National Television? She bought over $140 in groceries and only paid $7.04 because of coupons.

living during a period of national emphasis on physical fitness. Do you realize the stores of this nation will actually pay you to get exercise? That's right. You don't have to get up every morning and do jumping jacks with a TV fitness freak. (I don't like that guy; nobody can be that happy early in the morning. It has to be put on. Or he is really taping it the night before or some other time.) You don't have to belong to some health spa and pay $20 a month to do exercises either. The store will pay you.

How? Here's a can of string beans at eye level for 58¢ a can. On the lower shelves are string beans for 49¢. The store is paying you 9¢ per can to get in shape with a few knee bends.

The most expensive items of their kind are on the eye-level shelves where they are easy to see and reach. The comparable inexpensive products are on the lower shelves.

You say, "But what about quality?" That's a concern, of course. Often the 58¢ beans are not only just as good as the 49¢ beans but they are exactly the same product.

I got my eyes opened while doing an audit on inventory for a major food packer. I was there watching them put labels on the cans of string beans moving through the production line. A bell rang and the machinery stopped. A worker took the name-brand labels out of the machine and put in labels of a grocery chain. The machinery started again, now putting new labels on identical string beans.

Why spend 58¢ when you can buy the same thing for 49¢? Each and every one of the major food chains has its own house brand. These are quality products, and you can save up to 15% of your shopping dollar just by buying them instead of top brands.

Even beyond that, don't write off the cheap or generic

brands. Instead of getting a can of string beans, every one of which is an inch and a quarter long with a diagonal cut, some will be long and some short; you might get some halves and some end pieces. If you buy a can of cheaper peaches, instead of getting perfect halves or slices, you will get mixed and irregular sizes and shapes. Is that so bad?

Rule No. 7: *Understand unit pricing.* By unit pricing, we mean the comparative price per ounce (or other unit of measure). In other words, which is cheaper per ounce, the small size or the giant size? This brand or that brand? Which merchandising package is giving you the most for your money? Normally the "large economy size" is a better buy than the small or regular sizes—normally, but not always.

Of course, the producers usually don't make unit pricing easy for you. If they have a one-pound package, they won't have a four-pound package; it will be 4 lb. 7 1/2 oz. If they make an 11 oz. size, they won't have a 44 oz. size; it will be 57 oz.

Did you ever see a little man standing in front of a grocery shelf a long time, with his lips moving, a far away look in his eyes, and a puzzled half-frown on his brow? Mentally he's saying, "Now this smaller one is 1 lb. 2 oz. for 99¢ which is about uh, uh 5 1/2¢ an ounce, compared to this big one which is 3 lb. and 5 1/2 oz. (3 x 16 = 48 + 5 1/2) about 53 oz., divided by $2.88 which is uh, uh about . . . "

And by the time he works *that* problem, he's forgotten what his first per-ounce price was!

Happily some stores now post the per-unit price, which makes your task of comparing much simpler. And thanks to the revolution in electronic calculators, you can now buy an instrument for just a few dollars that will make unit pricing a snap.

In unit pricing canned vegetables I suggest you look

for a target price of 2¢ an ounce. That is about the best price you are going to find. Let's say you buy a house brand of string beans, 16 oz. cans, three for $1. Three times 16 is 48; that's 48 ounces for $1, just a little over 2¢ per ounce. That is a good buy. I suggest 2½¢ an ounce for frozen vegetables—peas, carrots, string beans, corn. Something exotic like artichoke hearts will cost more.

Rule No. 8: *Consider the per-serving price.* On most items the per-ounce price is the important thing, but on some items, go for a target price per serving. On fresh fruits and vegetables, try for 7¢ per serving. That means you are going to be buying smaller apples, for example, but you will also find fewer large uneaten apple cores underneath the sofa. Children don't eat those big things. You will also find that you as an adult are just as satisfied to eat a small apple or orange or banana as a big one, and it will be less calories for you.

Rule No. 9: *Avoid junk foods.* Often, the more a food is processed the more it costs and the less food value it has. Potatoes are really expensive when you have to pay 20¢ a pound for them in raw form, but if you buy potato chips those potatoes are costing you at least five times that much, and they aren't all that good for you either. An occasional snack is one thing, but such things as potato chips in the daily diet is quite another.

As pointed out earlier, we are a nation of dieters. One way to assure yourself a national best seller is to write a book about dieting. (I told my publisher we should capitalize on this, but he thought a book about finances could hardly be called the Accountant's Unbalanced Diet Book.) I have priced out many diets and would submit to you that the Weight Watchers plan is one of the most economical if the entire family is on it.

I know a number of readers will immediately want to write and challenge me on this, but I want to point out two things. First, the Weight Watchers plan actually entails less food because of the strict portion control, so there is very little wasted food. Second, you will not be buying any expensive junk food. You really can eat better for less if you want to.

Rule No. 10: *Go easy on prepared foods or so-called convenience foods.* Compare the cost of packaged pudding mix with canned pudding, for example. And what about gravy? It costs very little to make at home. Small snack cakes for lunches cost far more than a slice of home-baked cake or cookies. TV dinners, toaster waffles and pastries, ready-made pizzas—all cost more as a rule than the same items prepared at home, and often the quality is inferior too.

Rule No. 11: *Do comparison shopping.* Obviously with the price of gasoline what it is, you can't drive across town to save a nickel on a can of tuna. However, large grocery chains very often locate their stores in the same neighborhood, many times directly adjacent to each other. Shop for the specials at such stores. And don't overlook the independent supermarket in your neighborhood or on your travel route. Specials there are sometimes better than at the chain stores.

Rule No. 12: *Buy in quantity at super-bargain prices.* An investment in a food freezer or a frozen-food locker can result in significant savings for you, especially if you can find a good used inexpensive freezer.

I wouldn't recommend buying a side of beef to fill your freezer, nor would I subscribe to a freezer food plan. You will get better prices, and be buying the items you really want, if you simply shop the specials at your local meat outlets. But when you find a real bargain on fryers or hamburger or roast beef or whatever, don't buy just enough for one or two meals. Stock your freezer.

If you live in an area that grows abundant crops, you can probably fill your freezer with vegetables and fruits quite cheaply at peak-of-the-season prices. You can also buy "day-old" bread and other bakery goods at excellent savings. Once frozen and thawed, you won't be able to tell them from fresh.

Also you should begin stocking inventories of non-perishables that are on sale, especially toiletry items. It is an undeniable and eternal truth that when you are out of Crest, Crest is never on sale. So when you do find toilet items on sale, stock up. I am now in the market for razor blades because I am down to my last four or five packs. I bought fifteen packs of Wilkinson Blades, super stainless, at 47¢ each. I have a light beard, so each pack easily lasts me a week. Now I am looking for another sale. Why should I go out and spend 97¢ when I can get them on sale for 47¢? Coupon refunds are often available with blades.

Food prices are, if you will permit an understatement, subject to change. The principles outlined in this chapter will serve you well, even though prices will change considerably and certain marketing techniques (such as coupons, methods of labeling products, grading of meats, etc.) may vary.

To keep current with conditions in your area and to expand your capabilities for eating well at reasonable cost, avail yourself of the Extension Service near you. The Extension Service is a joint effort of your state government, county government, and the U.S. Department of Agriculture, in conjunction with colleges and universities. The services they offer are many and valuable.

Small study groups may be meeting monthly all over your area right now. An example of a year's program for such groups follows:

September	DRYING FOODS: Foods that dry well, how to dry in oven as well as dehydrator, storage, rehydration of dried foods.*
October	HOW TO HANDLE A HEALTH EMERGENCY: What actions you can take when a health emergency arises. Knowing what to do and when until help arrives.
November:	THIRTY-MINUTE MEALS: Tasty, nutritious meals that can be prepared in minutes at reasonable cost.
December	Free choice meeting.
January	ENERGY-SAVING COOKING TIPS: Energy cost comparison on use of different small appliances in the kitchen. Menu and recipe ideas.
February	LIFE WITH FATHER: The at-home husband, whether retired, unemployed, ill or temporarily disabled. Attitudes of husband and wife—family understanding.
March	CONSUMER BUYMANSHIP OF FABRICS: New fabrics in the market, costs, advantages and disadvantages and what to consider as far as care.
April	UNDERSTANDING SINGLE-NESS: In a changing society, many people find themselves "single," either through death of a spouse, dissolution of a marriage, or prolonged separation. Understanding feelings of singleness,

*Send $5 to my address at the back of the book and I'll send you directions on making a dryer for under $10.

May	whether they be yours or a friend's. THINK METRIC: How widespread is the metric system? Learn metric terms and measures. How to convert to "thinking metric" the easy way for use in the home.
Mini-Lesson:	OVER-THE-COUNTER-DRUGS— Selecting and using over-the-counter medications. What they can and cannot do. When to use and not to use.

Your participation in these neighborhood groups can both help you save money and also provide many opportunities to get to know people and to witness for Christ.

Many other services are also available through Extension, including correspondence courses, special interest programs, newsletters, consumer packets, and bulletins on a wide range of topics from your weekly food bill to starting and caring for a lawn.

Jacob, who lived through seven years of famine, said when he was old, "God . . . fed me all my life long" (Gen. 48:15). We can trust Him to feed us also, through times of scarcity as well as times of plenty. But we need to do more than simply trust; we need to act wisely. "Trust in the Lord, *and do good*; so shalt thou dwell in the land, and verily thou shalt be fed" (Ps. 37:3).

8

How To Stay Out of Debt
Despite BankAmericard

If you have credit cards, the first thing you should do is destroy them. Take a pair of scissors and cut them in half. Then put one half in the garbage under the kitchen sink, and put the other half in the bathroom waste basket, thereby avoiding any possibility of divine healing. Seriously, the main reason I want you to destroy them is that so often credit cards become the masters and we become the slaves.

Let's talk first about oil company credit cards. Everybody says, "Well, we pay the full bill each month, so we are not really going into debt."

Okay, but you are spending 32% more for automobile servicing, if you are using gasoline credit cards, than you would need to. Having the card induces you to buy everything for your car at the service station, where it costs most. A minor tune up—oil and filter change, new spark plugs, new points—will cost $40 to $120 at a service station. You will pay $2.25 a quart for the oil, which you could get at a discount store for 52¢ to 62¢* a quart. You will pay $2.75 each for spark plugs. On sale you might buy them for as little as 67¢ a piece and you can get them anytime for

---

*With a rebate coupon, I paid 32¢ a quart in August 1987.

89¢. You will pay $7.95 for the oil filter instead of $2.25 to $3.95.

Usually, if you buy a set of tires at a service station, they will be the most expensive set of tires you will ever buy. If you buy a battery at the service station, it will be a very expensive one.

I am not saying not to buy automotive products at service stations. I am not saying not to have service work done at the station. I am saying that you can save money if you do it yourself. Or you can buy your own spark plugs, oil, and filters, take them to the service station and pay the man to do the work. He will charge for labor, and instead of $40 the job will cost closer to $20. Now this takes a little bit of time, and I am not necessarily saying you should do it. I am saying you can save money doing it that way.

You see, the problem is that one doesn't think in terms of spending money when a credit card is laid down. A statement is mailed to you at the end of the month, when you do your bills, and you pay $27 a month to Greasy Oil Co. Since you have this payment anyway, it's easy to add $300 worth of tires and pay $34 a month. Something else goes wrong with your car, so you put repairs on the credit card, and your debts gets bigger and bigger.

Now, I have work done at service stations all the time, but every time I do, I recognize I am paying more than I need to pay. We have a choice. We are the stewards. We can spend the money God gives us any way we choose. Almost always I choose to save money when I can. In this particular area of car maintenance, my knowledge has been very limited. I did very well on "Fill 'er up and check the oil," but beyond that I was in unfamiliar territory. I finally decided to learn a little bit about car repair and maintenance. I have done a couple of small jobs on my own car now, and I am really rather pleased with myself.

I first tumbled onto the menace of credit cards about four years ago.* Toward the end of the year, I was going through my finances. We had run up a Penney's bill that year, and it had gotten out of control. I sat down and asked this question: Of these purchases, what did we really need and what could we have done without? The needs came to $48. The "could have done withouts" came to $613.

In analyzing how this happened, I perceived that the first thing I bought was a need. In fact, it was something I needed very badly. It cost $42, and I intended to pay that in full the next month. When payment time came, some other need was more pressing and I paid only $10, the minimum payment. During the next month, while walking through Penney's, I saw a couple of sale items that looked real nice. I bought them because I was already paying $10 a month and these purchases would only extend that a couple of months. Then Penney's staged a big sale, and we got a couple of other things. Then I changed jobs, and I thought I needed a couple of suits. So it went. We made almost $700 worth of purchases of which we really needed only about $48 worth.

I said, "Okay, that's it!" We didn't charge anything for almost a year and a half after that, trying to get our spending under control.

Then I went to using only one credit card, the BankAmericard.† (Master Charge is similar.) I used it for two reasons. First, I travel quite a bit and I don't like to carry large sums of cash. I could have used travelers checks to buy airline tickets, for example,

---

*This was in 1971.
†Now VISA and MasterCard

but they cost money.* There is also the small inconvenience of obtaining them. BankAmericard is handier and cheaper if you use it right.

Second, BankAmericard gave me a permanent record for business and tax purposes. When I would get back to the office, I would take the little customer's receipts out of my pocket and put them in a clip and file them.

The important thing is that each month I wrote a check to BankAmericard for 100% of the last month's purchases. That way I was not falling behind and getting into debt. That also meant I was not subject to any charges, so using the card did not cost me anything.

Right?

Wrong.

I tried to control and limit my credit-card purchases. I wanted to be the master and my credit card the slave. Even so, I made many purchases because I had the card that I would not have made otherwise.

Instead of nursing a hangover, I now do my income taxes on January 1. I normally have my taxes done by midnight of the first day of the year. I watch the football games and do income taxes. The year I was on only one credit card, I went through all my BankAmericard purchases, asking in regard to each one, "If you had not carried that credit card and had to either pay cash or write a check, would you have made this purchase?"

That is an interesting question to ask yourself. When you have cash in your pocket, the issue of spending is vivid. You feel it everytime you lay down the money. How many times have you carried a $20 bill in your pocket or purse for a week or more? Then you break it and it is gone. I don't know what

---

*There are now many places where travelers checks are free.

it is about $20 bills. Until you spend the first dollar, they seem to last forever. Once you spend the first dollar, the rest of it vanishes.

It is not easy to plunk down cash for any sizable purchase. It is a little easier to write a check because you don't quite see the money. You write down some figures; you have a $124 balance and you subtract $34 and now you have $90. It is even easier to slap down a credit card. But then, at the end of the month, it catches up with you.

What wouldn't I have spent? My answer was about $172 that year. I got some personal things using my BankAmericard because it was so easy. I didn't have the money, I didn't have the checkbook, but I had the card. I saw something I wanted, and I had been good that week, so I bought it. Let me cite an example of one of my "wouldn't have" purchases. I was in K-Mart, walking through the building supply section, and I saw a miter box. Now a miter box is a device that enables one to saw on angles. You know how everything comes together really nice on window and door moldings? That's accomplished by sawing the wood exactly on a 45 degree angle in a miter box.

I paid about $22 for a miter box and a small saw to go with it in October of 1973. I used it for the first time in November of 1974, to cut the moldings for a paneling job in our family room. In that period of thirteen months miter boxes were on sale at least three times.

Now, $172 is no big sum—the extra $15 a month in credit-card purchases didn't kill us. We could afford it. Perhaps you can too. But at least open your eyes to what can happen (and most likely does).

I have decided that for me credit cards are a trap, and I no longer use them.

Incidentally, in November of 1975 the Federal Trade Commission ruled that retailers may pass on to cash customers the savings realized by them when the bank credit cards are not used. You see, the retailer pays from 2 1/2% to 5% to the bank on every credit-card purchase. You can say, "Since I'm paying cash, will you discount the 3% you would have to pay if I used a credit card?" Often the merchant will agree.

Some people say, "But you will never be able to buy a house unless you have credit-card accounts, and you will have a terrible time cashing checks without credit cards to show." Not so. There are ways to establish credit without ever having credit cards or going into debt. One way to do it is by means of your utilities. Electricity, gas, heating oil—all can be put on what is known as equal pay or budget payment. The company estimates your annual usage, divides it by 12, and bills you the same amount each month. That establishes your ability to pay on a continuing basis. When someone runs a credit check, he is determining what is your ability to pay and what has been your record in making payments on time for obligations.

To further establish your credit, buy something at Penney's, Ward's, or Sears' on the "90 days as good as cash" plan. Although you have the money to pay cash, don't do it. Don't put it on their regular charge account plan either. Sign a contract, at no interest charge, to make a small down payment now, pay a third of the balance at the end of 30 days, another third at 60 days, and the remainder at 90 days. This establishes the fact that you are able to make payments.

Another method of establishing credit is to put some item on lay-away and make regular payments.

(On lay-away, you don't take the goods until you finish paying for them.) When creditors check that out, they see you had an obligation to pay $114, or whatever, and you paid it.

All of these things establish your credit. That, plus adequate income, is all you need to finance the purchase of a home.

As for cashing checks, large stores give identification cards for that specific purpose. These are not credit cards but will give you the privilege of cashing checks at that store. Banks also issue courtesy cards that may be accepted along with your driver's license as identification for check-cashing privileges.

You can get the benefits of established credit, then, without the liabilities of credit cards, and unless you are very sure you can manage credit cards better than I can, I'll stick with my original advice to cut them in two and hide the pieces.

A credit card too often becomes a license to spend money you can't spare for goods you don't need. That's one privilege you can very well do without.

Note

For those of you concerned that you have to establish credit to buy a house, don't worry. A home is a collateral loan, not a credit loan. You don't have to establish credit to buy a home.

9

How To Establish a Realistic Budget

I'd love to begin this chapter with a humorous anecdote, but I can't think of anything funny about budgeting. It is a totally unfunny subject. Budgeting is a pain. It's a hassle. At least, that is the attitude I often encounter. People think budgeting is a difficult project for accountants only, and they see it as a very constraining and legalistic system to have to live with.

In life, we find that when we establish boundaries we're much more comfortable. Isn't this true with our children? The child that is insecure and a discipline problem is the child that has never had boundaries. "Son, you can go this far, but no farther. You can stay out this late, but no later. You can go with these people, but not those people." These are boundaries. They give my son total freedom to move within these boundaries, but when he crosses the line, a corrective action will be taken.

"Son, what did I say about getting home at thus and so time?"

My son responds, "Well, Dad, you said to be home by 5 o'clock."

"Son, what time is it?"

"Well, Dad, it's now 6 o'clock."

Because my son is older my response at this point is, "Well, what are we going to do about that?"

Notice, it's a "we." I involve my son in this. And we'll set down some sort of corrective action: a spanking, a restriction, loss of privilege, whatever the case may be.

Now that's exactly what a budget is. A budget is setting down a series of rules or boundaries. I will spend so much money for food, but no more; so much money for a car, but no more. Then we live within these boundaries. We have total freedom to buy as much as we want in the way of clothing, for example, so long as we don't spend more than the $73 we have accumulated in our clothing fund. We are free to spend only $18 on vacation right now, because we've just taken a vacation and spent most of the money budgeted for that purpose.

If we over-spend in any area, a corrective consequence happens. This corrective consequence is called "not enough money." Most of us have ended up in that very uncomfortable situation—we have way too much month left at the end of the money. This, in essence, is a corrective action for going beyond the boundaries we set for ourselves.

I've heard individuals say, "Oh, boy, if I have to live on a budget, it's just not worth it. All that hassle to earn the money and then I have to watch where every penny goes. I just can't live that way."

What they're actually saying is, "I can't be disciplined." It's that same type of person who doesn't read his Bible, doesn't show up at church, doesn't allow the Lord to give him the input to take corrective actions in other areas.

To be totally disciplined, you need to govern all areas of your life—not only your Bible reading, your prayer life, and your Sunday-go-to-meeting life, but also your financial affairs.

The startling fact is that if you are not operating on a budget, you are wasting between $50 and $175 a month, depending on how much your income is and at what level you are spending.

If you are on a very low income you may be saying to yourself, "Oh, wow, I can't believe that. I make only $980 a month; if I wasted $50, I couldn't even get by." Yet, as we begin to look at a budget system, you will see that you should be setting money aside in certain areas and you are not doing so. One of the reasons you are not doing so is that you are wasting between $50 and $175 a month. I will stand by that statement.

I want to share now a budget form with you (see below). We said in Chapter 5 that one of the foundation stones on which to build a 'structure of financial freedom is tithing. So our budget form calls for 10% of your gross income to go to the Lord. I don't want this to be a source of bondage to anybody. If you have developed another system of giving that is satisfactory—it's something less than 10% of the gross, but you feel it's acceptable to the Lord and He is blessing—go ahead and continue it if you want to continue to be wrong.

Budget

Gross Income $_____

Fixed Expenses

    Income & Payroll Taxes $_____
    Social Security   _____
    Union Dues   _____
    Tithe (10% of Gross)   _____
    Other_____   _____
    _____   _____

Total Fixed Expenses $_____ $_____

Working Income (Deduct Total Fixed $ _____
          from Gross Income)

Budgeted %
  $ _____ Savings
       (10% of Working Income) $ _____

  $ _____ Living Expenses
       (75% of Working Income) $ _____

	Monthly	Per Pay Period
Mortgage or Rent	$ _____	$ _____
Heat	_____	_____
Electricity	_____	_____
Water/Sewage/ Garbage	_____	_____
Telephone	_____	_____
Car Insurance	_____	_____
Gasoline	_____	_____
Car Repairs	_____	_____
Recreation/ Entertainment	_____	_____
Newspapers/ Periodicals	_____	_____
Health Insurance	_____	_____
Life Insurance	_____	_____
Doctors/Medicines	_____	_____
Food/Household	_____	_____
Cleaning/Dry Cleaning	_____	_____
Clothes	_____	_____
Home Furnishings	_____	_____
Emergency	_____	_____
Christmas & Gifts	_____	_____
Vacation	_____	_____
Allowances	_____	_____
Other_____	_____	_____
_____	_____	_____
_____	_____	_____

TOTAL LIVING EXPENSE $ _____ $ _____

$ _____ Debts and Buffer (15% of Working Income)

    _____   _____
    _____   _____
    _____   _____
    _____   _____
    _____   _____

TOTAL DEBTS $ _____ $ _____

Say that your gross income is $1800 per month. (Of course, you will have to adapt this form to fit your own income.) All right, we take from that your tithe—$180. Let's say income taxes and social security come to $340 and that's the extent of your "fixed expenses." That makes your total fixed expenses $520. You now have $1280 left. This is what we call working income. Notice, if credit union payments are being deducted from your check, don't subtract them under fixed expenses; they come at the bottom of the form under debts.

To the far left of the form, it says "budgeted percentage." There are three lines below that. The first one lists 10%—savings. That means 10% of working income—so in our example we would put 10% of $1280 or $128 aside for savings. That's the ideal. You may not be able to set aside 10% right now, but set up an ideal first and work toward it; see what you can do. In young families, this money is often needed for house payments.

Second is living expenses—75% of working income. In this case 75% of $1280 is $960. The third line is for your debt and buffer fund—15% of working income, which in this case would be $192. This 15% debt is a basic lending institution standard. It doesn't mean that if you have less debt than that, you should go out and get $192 a month of payments. Instead, use that money as extra savings or to improve living expense items.

Saving with a Purpose

Now let's consider each of your "budgeted percentage" items more closely. First, when we start talking about savings, we need to be careful that we are not involved in savings strictly for the sake of savings, because that has some real problems. God warned His people to beware lest their accumulated wealth cause "thine heart [to] be lifted up, and thou forget the Lord thy God" (see Deut. 8:11-14).

I think that is one of my biggest problems in this area of savings. I get a little money in the savings account and then my accounting mind takes over and I tend to think, *Well, God, I don't need you this month because I have some extra money I can always fall back on.* God doesn't want us to have that attitude.

Time after time my little savings fund has been wiped out. Then I say, "O God, I am going to have to depend on you."

That's where God wants us. He says, "Believe in *me*. Let *me* meet your needs."

However, having some money put aside in savings has potential for good as well as evil. I want my savings to increase my ability to serve Christ. For example, I hear some missionary share a real need, and God witnesses to my heart that I should help. I want to be able to buy that vehicle that's needed. If I have money in savings, I can just write out a check and give it to them. Better yet, I can just give it to the pastor and let him present it to them, so they won't know I did it. I don't need the credit; I just want to know that I am able to help meet needs. But that means I must save some money.

Again, if we save for the sake of simply accumulating wealth, we err seriously. "But they that will be rich fall into temptation and a snare, and into many foolish and hurtful lusts, which drown men in destruction and perdition" (1 Tim. 6:9). The Bible teaches that covetousness is a form of idolatry (see Col. 3:5).

So save with a purpose—to be able to give to God's work when special needs arise. And save to be able to buy for cash, so that you won't be bogged down with debts. That way you won't be paying a lot of God's money for interest.

I believe there is a scriptural basis for putting a tithe of our income into savings toward the cash purchase of those things we desire.

> "You shall surely tithe all the produce from what you sow, which comes out of the field every year. And you shall eat in the presence of the Lord your God, at the place where He chooses to establish His name, the tithe of your grain, your new wine, your oil, and the first-born of your herd and your flock, in order that you may learn to fear the Lord your God always" (Deut. 14:22, 23, NASB).

Note that this "second tithe" was not given to support God's work. The people ate it themselves "in the presence of the Lord." It was a celebration of God's kindness and provision, a recognition that God was their benefactor.

Provision was also made, in case they lived far from the temple, to convert this tithe of their produce into money, which they could more easily carry. "And you may spend the money for whatever your heart desires" (v. 26). The necessary stipulation was that this tithe be consumed "in the presence of the Lord your God and rejoice, you and your household."

So save 10% of your income. Then when you can afford to buy something you desire for cash, rejoice and thank God for His kindness, and enjoy the product as a gift from His hand.

Your Cost of Living

Second, let's consider more closely the 75% of our working income dedicated to living expenses. Note the items listed on the budget form.

Mortgage or rent: If you are buying a house, your mortgage payments may include a property tax reserve and an insurance reserve. If not, be sure to list those expenses at the bottom of this column under "other."

Heat, electricity: You can put your yearly heat and electricity costs on an equal monthly payment plan. If you haven't done this, it might be a good idea. Utility and fuel companies would rather have you on equal payments than have to bill a large amount and only get part of it. And it can make it easier for you since you won't have any big bills to worry about. That's good.

Water, sewer, garbage: Just list the monthly sum.

Telephone: That's an interesting budget item. Advertising does such a wonderful job. You are sitting watching TV and on comes a commercial: "Remember how it was when you were back home with Mom and Dad? Long distance is the next best thing to being there." You run over to the phone, dial about 10 digits, and say, "Hi, Mom, it's your little boy. I'm calling long distance." All the time you are thinking, *Oh, boy this is going to cost me. I don't want to get this bill next month.* You planned to talk for only three minutes—that wouldn't cost too much—but you can't say, "Sorry, Mom, only two seconds to go on my three-minute call, bye!" So you talk for five or six minutes or maybe even fifteen or twenty-five or forty minutes. What did you say in that conversation that you could not have said in a letter for a fraction of the cost? You say, "But I really love these people and I want to show them how much I love them: It's so much nicer to call than just to write." Not really. It takes more effort, more giving of yourself to sit down and write a long letter than it does to just pick up the telephone and call. If you use long distance much, you could save a lot of money by calling less and writing more.

Car insurance: How much is your car insurance? Say, $45 a month? Most often we think in terms of car insurance as $270 every six months or $540 a year. That's $45 a month. If you don't put aside $45 every month when the car insurance comes due, where are you to get the $270? Chances are you will finance it, 10% down and eight months on the balance. So you pay $66 a month for eight months, and then what happens? You don't owe the $66 anymore so when you have occasion to buy a TV or some furniture, you figure you can handle the monthly payments and you buy it. What happens four months later? Your auto insurance comes due—$540. Do you have the money? No, so you go out and finance it again. See the pattern? You are always paying for things in arrears and paying a lot of money in interest as a result.

What you should be doing instead is setting aside so much each and every month. If you are financing your car insurance premium now and it is costing you $45, take another $8 a month and set it aside in a car insurance fund. You can afford an extra $8 a month; that's no problem. At the end of eight months don't discontinue payments. Take the $45 plus the $8 and put aside $53 a month into the car insurance fund. At the end of a year you will have $276 (8 × $8 plus 4 × $53), enough to pay half of your year's insurance premium in advance. Keep up your program of setting aside small sums and you will soon be on a complete cash system with all accounts current. Beautiful! What a feeling of freedom!

If you don't have liability insurance on your car, you should. God says you are to obey the laws of the land, and it is mandatory to have car insurance in many states. If you can't afford liability insurance, you can't afford to drive. Look for another way to get back and forth, say, get in a car pool. Or ask the

Lord to provide you the money to get insurance. *But don't drive without it.*

Maybe I seem a bit emphatic about this, but having worked in insurance I feel very strongly. I have looked at claim files with letters like this: "We are sorry. Your insurance expired two months ago. We advise you to get a lawyer."

Do you realize that when you incur personal liability due to an automobile accident, you are under a life-time obligation? Even bankruptcy will not absolve you from the actual dollar liability involved. They can garnish your wages for life to take care of that.

On the other hand, if you drive an older car worth under $1000, don't waste money on collision insurance. If you own the car outright, you aren't required to have insurance on it, and it really is not a good investment, especially if you are a careful driver and unlikely to have an accident that is your fault.

Gasoline, car repairs: You can figure out how much you spend on gasoline. For repairs figure $35 a month on a brand-new car, $60 on a car up to five years old, and $75 on a car older than five years.*

Recreation/entertainment: That's not an optional expenditure, men, nor can you spend it all on hunting and fishing or other pursuits that leave out the rest of the family. You must get your wife out of the house at least twice a month, get her away from the kids, and just be with her.

You say, "Now, wait a second. We are going on a tight budget. We are going to get out of debt and we won't have an extra $15 to put in a recreation fund."

If you try that, here is what will probably happen. For a few weeks, things may go great, but somewhere down the line trouble is waiting. One of the kids will

---

*A good average for both replacement and repair is 15.5¢ per mile.

get sick, or the car won't be working right, or there will be pressure on from some other source. That discouragement on top of the fact that your wife hasn't been out of the house for a month will make you say, "Oh, fooey, it's not worth it." You will grab your checkbook or credit card and go running out to dinner, with bowling afterward, topped off with a stop at the pizza parlor or ice cream shop. Bye, bye, budget. The next day you will feel miserable, guilty, and worthless. But you will probably do the same thing again because we are not built for constant, unrelieved pressure. We are built to get out and to get away from the grind occasionally.

So put something aside for recreation even if it's only $10 a month. That is not a lot of money but it will pay for babysitters twice. You don't have to go anyplace really exotic. Check your local newspaper for free events. If you live in a major metropolitan area, there are numerous such events. If nothing else, just go out for a drive or visit some special friends, or play games. The whole point is to meet your wife's need for some diversion.

Personally, I determined some time ago that I was going to make my wife my best friend. Do you know why I did that? My best friend came to town, and I changed my whole schedule around to be with him, to play tennis, to share what the Lord was doing in our lives—just to fellowship together. The next Tuesday evening I got a call from a desperate couple who needed some counseling. I was supposed to go out with my wife that evening, but I thought I'd simply telephone her and say, "Honey, look, these people really need me, so we'll have to put this off." I'm saying to myself, "She'll understand." But then I thought, *No, she won't understand; she has been planning on this for a month and a half. If I was willing to change my whole schedule last week just to be with my best friend, why am I going to shuffle my wife way down the list?*

At that point I made a commitment to try to do one thing each week just a little bit different to tell my wife I loved her. It has really been fun. One week it got clear down to Friday and I had forgotten to do anything. Here I was, flying to California and not coming back until Sunday night. The plane made one 20-minute stop en route, so I ran into the terminal and got Meg a card. On the front it said YOU KNOW HOW MUCH I LOVE YOU? And inside was this little guy with widespread arms and a silly grin saying THIS MUCH. I just signed it and said, "I miss you, Love, Malcolm."

I was delayed in California and didn't get back home till Wednesday. By then I had forgotten all about the card. When I came in, Meg threw her arms around me, gave me a big hug, and said, "Thank you! I *loved* getting your card!" Right in the middle of a very hectic schedule I had taken time to remember her. It is important, men, that your wife know she is No. 1 in your life after God.

You say, "Oh, she knows that."

No, she doesn't—not unless you tell her; not unless you show her on a continuing basis.

Now, let me tell you men a valuable secret. I got onto this completely by accident—in fact, I stumbled onto it. Flowers work wonders with women. You know, I get my favorite meals all the time. Maybe I come home early to mow the lawn; the lawn has already been mowed. Maybe I'm going to spread a half unit of bark dust; it's all spread. No reason for Meg to do these things except to let me know she loves me, too, and to take some pressure off me. It's fantastic.

I discovered the power of flowers in an office situation. I had a rip in the seam of my coat down the back, and this woman who had a couple of sons almost my age spotted it. She said, "Take it off and I'll sew it up," which I did and she did. While out to lunch that day, I passed a flower shop. I enjoy going into flower shops just to look around; I love the arrangements and the smell. So I went in, and there were six baby roses with some ferns for $1.98—I think they were a day old. I thought, *Hey, I'll buy those for Ella*, because I really appreciated her taking time to mend my coat. Back at the office, Ella took one look at those roses, tears sprang to her eyes, and she went dashing out of the room. I thought for sure I had done something wrong. But I found out I had done something right. Those were the first flowers Ella had ever received in her entire life. I tell you, I was a hero around that office for weeks.

When I saw the tremendous effect of those flowers, my practical male mind took over and I thought, *Potted flowers would be better because then she can keep them indefinitely*. Then I thought, *Artificial flowers would be even better; they can't die*. But, take it from me, plastic ones do not work. Only the cut ones are sure dynamite. I think it's because they are so completely impractical—their function is totally aesthetic. This says to a woman, "I love you, I care, I am willing to 'throw money away' for you." I don't know for sure what it is, but I do know they work.

You might be saying, "Why, if I were to bring flowers home, my wife would say, 'What has he been up to?' "

Just let her think or say that. She may hassle you, "We can't afford those; why did you buy them?" But if you could be there the next morning, you would see her call up her mother, her aunt, her sister, and maybe her hairdresser to share the news. Try it, men; you'll really like it; *she'll* really like it. It works.

Newspapers/periodicals: Don't subscribe to publications you never read. And consider the possibility of picking up newspapers at the stands only on the days you really want them. As for periodicals, could you as easily borrow them from the public library?

Health insurance, life insurance: I am not planning to get sick and I don't intend to die before I am seventy or eighty years old, so why do I have health insurance and life insurance? I am not going to get into an automobile accident, so why do I have car insurance? Okay, I want to deprive Satan of any basis of attack. I know the spirit of my wife is such that though she doesn't expect any of us to get sick, she feels a lot more secure knowing it wouldn't wipe us out if we did because we have health insurance. There is no way for Satan to prey on doubts in our minds this way. He has absolutely no ammunition.

I have talked to many couples who are uninsured and the husband is not worried but the wife has a little doubt. Remember, the wife is looking at the short-term. She is looking at her house that has no mortgage insurance on it, and she knows there is no way she could make those monthly payments if something happened to her husband. Satan has some ammunition to use against her right there. But if you have insurance, you can say to Satan, "Get out of here; it's taken care of."

Doctors/medicines: This is not to pay the bills you already have but to set a little money aside.

Food/household: That's a tough one. Figure perhaps $70 to $150 a month for each person aged 14 and over, $65 to $130 for those aged 9 to 13, about $80 for those aged 4 to 8, and from $40 to $85 for those under age 4. Now this is only for food; you must add for cleaning supplies, paper goods, toothpaste, and the like.

How a family of five with one of them being a teenager can get by on less than $240 a month, I don't know. I know some women are doing it, but you know, men, you really need to take some of the pressure off your wives in this area and begin to give them adequate household allowances. They are having to skimp; as a result they never have the extra money to take advantage of the bargains—to buy three cases of corn when it comes on sale, for example. If she were to invest enough money of the inadequate amount given her to buy three cases of corn, you would be eating corn every night for the next three months because she wouldn't have money left for anything else. But buying bargains in quantity would save you money in the long run and provide a better diet for the family. An active garden can cut these costs greatly.

Cleaning/dry cleaning: I combine this item with food/household.

Clothes: What I do is tell the Lord my needs. I told the Lord I needed suits that would still look fresh after a four-hour flight, because I get off the airplane and go speak to a group of people. That requires suits of fairly good quality. The general price range of such suits is $90 to $250. But I said, "Lord, you know the type of suit I need, but I don't want to spend that kind of money. I want to buy my suits for under $30.* So you just provide them for me." And God does.

I have two suits that cost me $19.88 each, two

---

*My last suit for under $30 was May 1983. As of 1987, I've finally lifted my level to $50. Inflation has finally hit my suits.

that cost me $24 each, a couple that were $29.88 each, and one that I paid $59 for—and that one has a story behind it. Last summer I was going through Penney's and I found this beautiful grey suit. I mean, it was so gorgeous, and I got the worst case of "I want." I wanted that suit so badly I could taste it. Originally $80, it had been marked down to $59. I said, "That's neat, Lord; it's already on sale at a real savings."

This little voice said, "Didn't you say that you wanted them under $30?

I said, "Okay, Lord, fine; you'll provide my needs—but I need that one."

I went home but my mind stayed at Penney's. After a while I said, "Hey, Meg, how would you like to go out and do some shopping? We do need some shoes and some other things for the kids." So we got in the car and somehow ended up at Penney's. Guess what? The children's shoe department was right next to the sale rack for men's suits. Wasn't that a coincidence?

I said, "Hey, Meg, take a look at this suit." She looked at it and said, "Oh, that's just perfect for you; that's really nice." *Ah, confirmation from the Lord that I am to get it,* I thought.

"Well, it's $59," I said. "Do you think that's too much?"

"No, it's an $80 suit, but I thought you kind of had an agreement with the Lord that you would buy them under $30."

I said, "Yes, that's right. That's true. Well, okay, we'll just let the Lord provide, then." So we went over and started looking through shoes and I said, "You know, that's really a bargain, and that is an awfully nice suit for $59. I bet you the Lord might really want me to reconsider. Listen, if God wants me to have that suit, He can provide a shirt and tie on sale that are just perfect for it and that will be His affirmation that I should get that suit."

You know, it only took me three and a half hours to find a shirt and tie that matched that suit. The whole time I was trying to justify myself in making the purchase. I bought the suit for $59.

Three weeks later I was in Penney's, so I stopped by the sale rack. There was an identical suit, my size, and it had been marked down to $52. I said, "O Lord, you're not!" And as soon as I said that, I said, "Oh, yes, you are. You are going to take that suit and run it right down below $30, and it's going to be my size, and I could have had it that way." So God taught me a little lesson.

You see, I can afford to go out and spend $200 on a suit. God has given us as a family enough income for that sort of thing. But I see no reason to spend all that money when I can spend $30 and give the other $170 to the Lord. I would much rather take that extra money and give it to His work. Last year God enabled us to give almost $1000 this way over and above our tithes and offerings. We said, "Lord, if you provide this, we will send the extra to you." He provided and we sent the extra.

Home furnishings: The Lord taught me a lesson in this area also. Our refrigerator went on the blink. I checked and it was plugged in, so I called out the repair man. He looked it over, said the compressor was shot, and announced it would cost $175 to repair it. I didn't have $175,* and those guys don't accept terms; you pay them when they walk out the door.

I really couldn't even afford to go to a garage sale right then, and, wouldn't you know it? The washing machine picked the same time to conk out. We had bought the washer six years before for $25 at a garage sale, so we couldn't complain about it.

---

*In September 1983, we spent $480 on a compressor and repairs of a refrigerator/freezer. The replacement would have been $1400!

But here I was up against some big expenses for which I had no cash.

"Well, we will just have to buy them on time payments," we decided. So we went out to get new appliances. We discovered they didn't make the great big refrigerator/freezer combinations anymore. They made small side by side ones, but nothing as big as we were used to. So we just had to have a freezer too. We ended up buying a washer, a refrigerator, and a freezer—all on time.

We paid $10 down; that brought the balance to $700, with payments of $23 a month. That was about the first of November and we had 45 days before the first payment was due.

Early in December I get a little notice in the mail: "Because of your excellent payment history [I hadn't paid a penny!], we are going to allow you to skip a payment to have the extra money you need at Christmastime."

Wonderful. I was going to spend extra money at Christmas anyway, so I signed the little card and they skipped a payment and just added the interest. I knew that 22% interest was a little steep, but I'd double up my payments soon; and when I got my income tax refund, I would pay off the whole thing, so I wasn't too worried about the cost.

As it turned out, I made my payments every month—no doubles and no pay off. Comes the next December and I get this little card in the mail inviting me to skip a payment at Christmas. I sat down and figured it out. I had made 11 payments of $23 a month, a total of $253 on an original balance of $700, and my outstanding balance was still $618. Then I projected ahead on the same payment schedule and discovered that because I did not have $175 to repair an otherwise perfectly good refrigerator/freezer combination, and some cash for a washer, it was going to cost me over $1400 to buy those appliances. That is bad stewardship in anybody's book. I was paying twice what the appliances were worth. I said, "Never again!"

This budget item, then, is for setting aside funds so we will be prepared for these expenses that will occur. When you buy a brand-new house, eventually that built-in stove is going to be replaced. The garbage disposal will probably have to be replaced too. These things are going to wear out. So set money aside for just this purpose.

Emergency: I call this my emergency/yahoo fund. When I get to the end of the year and haven't had any emergencies, I have something else I want to spend my money on, and I go, "Yahoo!"

Christmas and gifts: You will spend money at Christmas. I don't care how many of your gifts you make, you will spend money. Set aside $10 a month and at least you will have $120 so you can buy a turkey, decorations for the tree, wrapping paper, postage stamps, cards. It's going to cost.*

Vacation: The most fun vacation I ever took in my life was last April.† I paid cash for everything and came home with cash left in my pocket. Fantastic. Not once during the entire vacation did we say, "We can't afford this. How will we ever pay for it when we get home?" We paid for it then and there. What a great feeling to come back from vacation and not owe a thing.

Allowances: Definitely provide allowances for your children. It's part of their training in both money management and faith. Since I deal with this at length in a separate chapter, I will not go into it here.

Other: List all regular and incidental expenses not included under any other heading. Be sure to in-

---

*The average family spent over $600 for Christmas 1986.
†April 1975 and all on cash since!

clude once-a-year or one-time expenses along with your regular monthly bills. For example, how much is the annual automobile license renewal in your state? How much per year do you need for the dog's license or for club dues? All of my little incidentals average about $8 to $9 a month. If I am not setting aside that amount each and every month, I can't pay these expenses when they arise. I have to take it out of food money, and the grocery budget gets hit hard enough by inflation without reducing it further. So difinitely include a sum here even if you must estimate it.

Handling Your Debts

Note that the third major designation of a percentage of your working income (15%) is for a debt and buffer fund. Here's how it works. First, make a list of all your debts. Suppose you have a bank loan of $500, a car loan of $800, a TV loan of $200, a personal loan of $500. The total is $2000. You have $192 (15% of your $1280 working income) available to make the payments for these loans.

Next, figure what percentage of your total debt is represented by each debt. In our example, each $500 debt is 25% of the total $2000. The $800 debt is 40% and the $200 debt is 10%.

Now multiply the money available ($192) by the same percentages. You have $48.00 (25% × $192) per month available for each $500 debt. You have $19.20 (10% × $192) for the $200 debt, and you have $76.80 40% × $192) for the $800 debt.

Now you really flip out because your combined payments are already, say, $252 a month, so how can you possibly operate on a debt-reduction budget of $192?

Okay, what you do is go to your creditors and say

something like this: "I have come to the place in my spiritual life where I realize I have been a bad witness in my payments of my bills. Here is my budget. I have worked it all out, and I have $192 that I can pay on these bills. I am going to each of my four creditors [or 7 or 12 or whatever the case may be], and I am asking them to take a reduced payment until I get my financial house in order." Assure them that you will pay them, but it will be a little slower than scheduled because if you don't organize your finances along this line, you are going to have to default somewhere.

I have found almost invariably that creditors are willing to do this if you have not previously made all sorts of rash promises and failed to keep them. If you have been juggling creditors back and forth—promising to pay by the 15th, getting another phone call on the 20th and telling them you'll have it there on the 25th, and finally giving them half of what you promised—one more promise from you is not going to do much good.

In a case like that, I would suggest you ask a Christian brother to counsel with you and to work as an intermediary. I help people this way quite often. I write to creditors on my CPA letterhead indicating the amount the debtor has available and the monthly payment he can handle. Most creditors cooperate because they can see the debtor is really trying to straighten out.

There are various consumer organizations and credit counseling agencies operating on a nonprofit basis. They will help you in various ways. Some will work out a budget with you and then receive a lump sum monthly from you, pro rating it to your creditors. That may not be your best alternative if all you are doing there is exchanging several creditors for one.

You may not really learn the lessons you need to learn. There is something very humbling about having to go personally to several creditors, confess your failings, and ask for terms. Once you have worked your way out of that situation, you will never want to get into it again. You will stick to better procedures from then on.

Keeping Track of Your Funds

We have been talking in this chapter about various funds for various purposes, and you may be trying to envision exactly how this works. Some of our grandparents used envelopes. Each payday they put aside money into the rent envelope, the phone envelope, the repairs envelope, the doctors envelope, and so on. I am talking about something similar; but instead of keeping it in cash sitting on a shelf, utilize a bank account and keep the funds separate only in your own accounting.

For example, suppose your budget called for the following monthly funds:

Auto insurance—$40
Doctors and medical—$30
Christmas and gifts—$25
Car repairs—$60
Furnishings—$25
Vacation—$30
Clothes—$20

That totals $230 per month. You get paid the first of each month, so on January 1 you deposit $230 in savings, and you show it as outlined above. On February 1, you make a second deposit of $230. You now have $460 in savings, and double the amount shown for each fund. Let's say in the middle of February you need to buy new shoes for two children and they cost you $30. You show a $30 withdrawal from the clothes fund. You now have $430 in savings.

On March 1 you add another $230 and your total becomes $660.

On March 10 your insurance premium comes due and it is $240. You show for 3/10 a $240 withdrawal from the insurance fund. You now have $420 left in savings, and your records show that you are $120 in the hole on the car insurance fund, with $90 in the medical fund, $75 in Christmas, $180 in car, $75 in home furnishings, $90 in vacation, and $30 in clothes.

What you have done, in effect, is to borrow from yourself. Instead of financing that car insurance premium and paying 22% interest, you have borrowed from your own funds.

Over the year, if your budget was realistic, the car insurance fund will come back into balance as you keep putting $40 into it each month with nothing coming out. You can get ahead of the situation too. Suppose that all of a sudden the Lord gives you some increase. Keep half for some fun and pay the car insurance fund back with the rest.

A good budget, then, can be a great aid to managing your money efficiently. Don't look at your budget as a nuisance or a necessary evil. It can be one of the best paper friends you will ever have.

As a tool, I have created *Financial Planning Guide for Your Money Matters.* This has all the forms you need to work out a budget as well as additional savings hints. If you would like to secure a copy, see page 176 for ordering instructions.

PART IV

Strengthening the Family
Through Right Use of Money

10

Father as Head of Family Finances

Remember the imaginary visits we made to a number of homes where husband and wife were engaged in disputes? We observed then how common it is for domestic discord to revolve around money. That was probably no news to you, for you could likely have supplied similar examples yourself, examples much more painful than those we shared because you personally live them.

I also described how God honored me when I specifically chose to put my family ahead of my business on one occasion, and I have emphasized the necessity of keeping the proper perspective in our lives: God first, family second, and vocation third.

Because of my concern for the family, and because money has such corrosive power to injure and warp the family—if not actually to destroy it—I want to draw your attention now to the possibilities of blessing and strengthening the family through the right use of money. Jesus is our Redeemer, and when we follow Him in all our ways, He redeems us from the potential curse of money and transforms our money into a blessing.

The very first thing many families need is to establish the husband as the budgeter and payer of the bills. I know some women readers are saying, "Oh boy! That's what got us in the mess to begin with; why, he can't handle a thing!"

Let me explain a few things about this. I have counseled with many women who every month go through the hassle of paying the bills, and it causes them worry, frustration, and problems. If you, as a wife, are solely responsible in your family for preparing the bills and this is causing you worry and frustration, then you are assuming responsibility that God never intended you to have. That's all worry is, as Bill Gothard says: Assuming responsibility that God never intended you to have.

What you need to do is to recognize that your husband has this privilege of handling the finances for the family. You see, God very creatively fashioned two different types of beings: Male and female. He created the male to have a general overall long-range viewpoint in matters concerning the family. When the husband gets to the end of the month and is $15-$20 short of paying all the bills, he is not terribly concerned because he has a bonus coming next month or something else is happening whereby he expects to balance things. He applies the general, logical mind the Lord gave him to meet that problem.

The wife, on the other hand, has a tendency to react to such problems from an emotional standpoint. Her frame of reference is the household. The fact that the electric bill might not get paid is a direct threat to her. The electricity might be shut off, and then how will she cook the food and keep her babies warm? That's her viewpoint.

Don't interpret this statement as a slam against women! Quite frankly, I've found that very often the wife is more capable of handling the bills than the husband. What I am trying to convey is that the husband needs to be made part of the "team" effort of getting the bills paid. Who handles the bookkeeping is not important; the importance is involving both husband and wife.

I have talked with women who have literally cried for two hours over the inability to pay a $5 bill. Such anxiety is not what God intended for these women. God intended for the husband to handle these things. If you are a woman reader and the handling of the bills doesn't cause any frustration, go ahead and continue; but, if it causes those frustrations, you need to go to your husband and say, "Honey, God is showing me that it is in the area of your authority to prepare the bills every month, that He intended you to lead our family because of your ability to handle these things, and I am to respect that authority."

Notice that you don't say he's been neglecting his responsibility, and he'd better shape up and do as God says. You talk in terms of his authority and privilege and leadership. Then you say, "I have really come to the place where I am going to bow out and let you take care of these bills. I am not going to usurp your authority anymore."

The husband may immediately object. He doesn't want this change because it involves taking a responsibility that he was previously able to avoid. It's comfortable for many men to have their wives take this responsibility. It will cause conflicts and problems in other areas, but many husbands will just avoid a lot of hassle by coming home, handing their wives their paychecks, and saying, "Now you take care of the bills." Husbands who do that are also the ones who come home with such newsy tidbits as, "By the way, I bought a new motorcycle; it's $18 a month; you take care of it." Or "Hey, I need a new set of golf clubs; I am going to get them; you take care of it."

Whether your husband is a Christian or not, God has established him as the leader. So go to your husband and say, "I really want to submit to your leadership."

He may say, "Okay, if you are so submissive, I deem in my role as leader that *you* are going to pay the bills."

That's fine, be submissive. Do exactly that. Next time you pay bills and come up short, list them all, go to your husband, and say, "Honey, we have $418 and the bills come to $490 [or whatever]; which bills don't you want me to pay?"

Don't you make that decision; ask him which bills you are to leave unpaid. If he says for you to decide, say, "Honey, I really can't. I don't know which ones. I really need your counsel and help on this. I recognize that God is going to make the decision through you. Which ones shouldn't I pay?"

He may say, "Look, if I am the leader, I say you make that decision."

"Okay," you reply, "I won't pay these last four." What you have done is to take his motorcycle and snowmobile and car and put them at the bottom of the list.

"No," he says, "wait a second—not those—make sure you pay those."

"But which ones shall I not pay, Hon?"

And all of a sudden he has to enter the act to protect some of his things.

Now, you must also mean business about respecting your husband's leadership. You must be willing to recognize that God is going to work His best plan through him. That means things are probably going to get worse before they get better. Think of the position in which you may find yourself. You get a phone call and the guy says, "This is the Acne Collection Company. How come you haven't paid anything on your 44-year subscription to Money Management Magazine for the past five months?"

"I'm sorry, that's not my responsibility; you'll have to talk to my husband," you reply.

Next, here comes a guy from the power company and he says he's going to collect the $58 you owe on the power bill or turn the electricity off, one or the other. You say, "Well, that's not my responsibility; I'll show you where the box is." So he shuts off the electricity. When your husband comes home, that's bound to remind him that he forgot to pay the power bill! I mean, even if you have dinner by candlelight, he's going to notice something's wrong sooner or later.

Now, wives, you have a chance here either to make it or break it. You will completely destroy any good work you have done if you attack as soon as he's in the door: "See, the kids are freezing to death, we'll all starve, the food we have will soon rot—all so you can have your stupid motorcycle!"

"I told you so!" Take those four words out of your vocabulary.

Instead, with a quiet, loving spirit meet your husband at the door, and say, "Hi, Hon, the man came out and turned off the electricity, but it's okay. I went next door and I was able to borrow what I needed to cook your dinner, and everything's ready." Be nice and loving and you will drive him out of his mind, because he won't be able to escape from his guilt into a hassle with you.

I know by experience how this works. One time I was supposed to be home at 6 p.m. and I came in the door at 8. I hadn't telephoned or anything and I was really without excuse, but while driving those last miles home I practiced my arguments until no matter what she came up with, I had a come-back. I was really ready.

I came walking in the door and she said, "Hi, Hon, no accidents? Everything okay? Great, I kept dinner warm for you, so why don't you come on now and eat?"

I thought she would holler at me, throw something at me, call me names, but *not* be so nice! I have never been late without calling again. I don't want to incur that guilt again for anything. It was terrible.

The whole thing is that we have to balance our personal guilt with blame we can lay against someone else. Go to a psychiatrist with guilt and what will he probably do? He can't take care of our guilt, so he tries for a mental balance by giving us more blame. "Your mother took away your teddy bear when you were two." Blame. "Your dad never went to Cub Scouts with you." Blame. "You brother didn't make your bed for you after you made his bed three days in a row." Blame.

That is exactly what Meg was not doing to me. I had plenty of guilt and I was ready to pile on the blame, but she didn't give me a chance. So I went out of balance and had to deal with my guilt, which, thank God, is taken away through God's provision for our forgiveness in Christ.

Perhaps as you read this, your situation is just the opposite, the husband handles everything and the wife knows nothing of the family finances. Husbands, you are losing a valuable resource by not consulting your wife! At our house, even our three children sit in on family budget conferences.

Establish the husband as the head of your family finances. It is my conviction that God's plan calls for husbands and fathers to exercise headship. And you can't improve on God's plan.

11

The Working Mother—Does It Pay?

Let me tell you a tale of two couples. Our first couple, a case of boy meets girl in church, has a happy beginning. Her parents are not Christians and they are a bit concerned about the hippy life-style of some of these Jesus freaks they have heard about. They are not so sure about their new son-in-law—he *does* have long hair, and their daughter has always enjoyed the nicer things in life. To insure that the kids start out right, her parents make the first and last months' payment on a $875-a-month apartment and sign a lease, which they give to the kids for their wedding present.

Of course, the kids also get a whole raft of beautiful wedding gifts. They can't occupy a beautiful $875 apartment and properly display and use all these beautiful gifts without some furniture, right? They go down to Levitz and get a bedroom set, a living room set, and a dining room set. The payments are only $98 a month, and they are both working so they can afford it.

Meanwhile, her car is old and sort of on its last leg, so they have to get a new car, but they can afford that too because they are both working.

And they did go on a honeymoon. They didn't have the money for it, but they put it on the Bank-Americard. They are able to handle those payments too because together they have a pretty good income.

Now they are going down the path of marriage and everything's fine for the most part. At year's end, they renew the lease on the apartment, and here they are sixteen months later.

You know, God has a beautiful plan for marriage, and it doesn't stop with "leave your father and mother and cleave unto your wife." That's not the end of the plan. God also said, "Be fruitful and multiply." So all of a sudden sixteen months later, our couple is saying, "Now, what are we going to do? We can't afford this baby." She can't quit her job because they must have her $1075 a month or they can't make their payments.

Worry, worry, fret, fret. You know, God has a beautiful solution to this problem, and it's called *prevention.* Not indefinite prevention of pregnancy through better contraceptives, but prevention of debt through application of better financial principles.

Now consider our second couple. She does quit work about eight months after their marriage and they have a family. Seven years later we look in on them. They have two pre-schoolers and one in school. All along God has been meeting their needs. Sometimes they have been squeezed, but a Christmas bonus or a raise or a new job has always been just enough to meet the financial crisis. For this they give God the honor and praise.

Now, however, the squeeze is really on, and it doesn't look as if there is any solution. He has recently switched jobs, so he can't switch jobs again. He just got a raise and he won't get another one soon. It's the middle of July so a Christmas bonus is a little bit chancey. What is he going to do?

About that time the wife says, "Listen, I can always go back to work at the bank for eight months until we're able to get out of this financial squeeze."

That is not the biblical answer.

A Case of Dollars and Sense

"The faster I go, the behinder I get." Some people have found themselves on that sort of frustrating treadmill. And it can easily happen to the family when mother goes out to work to catch up financially.

To build a case study, let's assume we have a mother and two pre-school children who are going to need babysitting while she works on a full-time job. The first thing our working mother is going to want is a wage, so let's assume it is $250 a week.* Now this comes out to $6.25 an hour, and I know some women wish they'd get that much, while others get more than that. We're talking about the average working mother who has gone through high school, maybe had a year working in the bank, and is a clerk typist or filing clerk. We're not talking about an executive secretary who can command $2,000 or more a month.

Now, out of that $250 weekly wage must come the added expenses. The first added expense a working mother must face is *taxes*. And those taxes are likely to be about $80 a week. The second expense is the *tithe*, ten percent of the gross, which in this case would be $25. Now you'll notice here that Uncle Sam doesn't take the same chance that God does.

---

*This wage and the expenses detailed later in this chapter are based on 1987 rates. As wages increase, expenses will rise too, so the conclusions will remain valid. We are assuming 2 children and a husband who earns $18,000 per year, so their combined salaries are just over the 1986 median family income of $29,458.

God allows you to *bring* the tithes into the storehouse; the IRS *takes* theirs before you even get your check.

The third expense is for *transportation*. This can be a very costly item. If you can join a carpool and get by for under $10 a week, you're fortunate. If you can take mass transit for a comparable cost, fine. Because of the hassle of having to get the kids to the babysitters or for other reasons of convenience, most working mothers end up driving a car downtown to the office or out to the plant. Now whenever you add another car you add expenses: insurance, gas and oil, repairs, maintenance, perhaps even car payments if you have to buy another car.

If you are going to have to drive to work, take a long look at the costs. For example, how much should you figure a month for repairs on a brand-new car? You say, "Nothing, it's under warranty, almost everything is taken care of. Oh, we could put $3 a month into an emergency fund just in case something not covered goes wrong during the first 12,000 miles."

Wrong. You should figure $35 a month for repairs on a new car, because the minute you start driving, your tires start wearing. Not only will your tires need replacement but so will spark plugs, filters, and fan belts. Eventually the brakes are going to need relining, the shocks and the exhaust system replaced, and a new battery installed.

You can do one of two things. You can either begin putting money aside ahead of time so that when the tires wear out you can plunk down $320 for a new set of four radials, or you can go along saying, "This new car isn't costing me anything."

When you suddenly need $320 worth of tires and don't have the money, you can use your Firestone credit card or your BankAmericard, or whatever, and begin paying $14 a month on those tires. You know how long those tires are going to last? Just about long enough to pay them off, so you will have to incur another $320 debt to replace them. You either get yourself ahead of the game or you get yourself behind, one or the other.

If Mom is going to drive to work, recognize that it's going to cost money. Figure $35 a month to maintain a new car, $60 a month on a car two to five years old, and $75 a month on a car more than six years old. And don't forget, if you have to rent parking space, that's going to cost something. The cheapest lot in downtown Portland is $85 a month.*

As an average, then, let's figure transportation will cost the working mother $26 a week.

Next, figure what you will spend extra for *lunch*. This can be debated. I'm including the coffee and roll that you buy in the morning and the coffee and ice cream (or piece of pie or candy bar) you have in the afternoon. I suggest $2.50 a day or $12.50 a week for this (obviously, more, if you eat out every day).

"Wait a second," you say "I've got that beat because I take a sack lunch." Okay, for you $7.50 may be a little high, but don't forget the coffee breaks. More important, probably twice a month the girls are going to decide to go out to lunch: somebody's getting married, somebody's leaving, somebody's going to have a baby, somebody's getting a divorce—well, anyway, there's *something* to celebrate. So you are all going out to lunch. I've been downtown many times and seen a table of seven girls out to lunch. Now they don't get together and say, "Listen, we're all down here working for some extra money to put in the family budget, so let's go to MacDonald's." That's not what they say. They pick out one of the most expensive places in town and shell out $4.25 for a tuna salad sandwich. So $12.50 for lunches is quite low actually.

---

*Hertz figures it costs 58¢ a mile to drive a mid-sized American car 10,000 miles a year for 3 years. For an extra 100 miles a week, a new car would cost $58 in 1987.

Next comes *restaurant carry-outs*. You know, "You deserve a break today," so you stop at Mac-Donald's and pick up a bag of hamburgers for the family's evening meal. Or you go to Shakeys and pick up a pizza. Maybe you buy a bucket of Kentucky Fried Chicken.

You say, "But I wouldn't do that. I'd fix our meals as I do now."

Maybe. But take a look at your schedule, Mom. You now have three full-time jobs: wife and mother, homemaker, and working girl. You are getting up at 6 o'clock in the morning to get all the kids ready so that you can put them in the car by 7 so that you can get them to the babysitter by 7:15, then downtown to park the car, up to the office, and ready to work at 8 a.m.

All day long you're picking up the phone, sweetly greeting people who grouch and snarl at you. It's not your fault, but the salesman from Prineville is bawling you out because he didn't get his order. You had nothing to do with it. You simply picked up the phone and said good afternoon and he laid right into you. But you have to smile and be nice to people in and out of the office.

You get off at 5 p.m., fight the traffic all the way to the babysitters, grab the kids, run to the store, dash in real quick, grab a couple of things, dash back out. It's now 6:30. You are home and now you are going to spend your loving time and care every evening preparing a beautiful dinner? No way. Restaurant carryouts come in at about $18 a week.*

How about extra *clothes*? I've talked to single girls and married ones, both older and younger, and I've struck $9.00 a week as an average. This is based on the assumption that you are not going to wear the same clothes downtown in an office situation that

---

*A national study forecasts that more than ½ of a family's food budget will be spent eating out by 1985—this because over ½ of all mothers work. Update—in 1987, 68% of all mothers with children under 18 are in the work force.

you wear cleaning the house. You want to make a nice appearance and be a good witness, and so you have to dress well.

You may say you will never spend anywhere near $9.00 a week.* Well, sit down and think about it. Besides the basic wardrobe, think of the extra shoes, handbags, summer and winter coats you will need. And what about pantyhose? How many pairs of pantyhose will you go through a week working? You know filing cabinets have this interesting little quirk; unless they have at least a weekly sacrifice of pantyhose, they stick. If one of those filing cabinets is stuck, all you do is snag your nylons and immediately they open. They must have them.

Maybe you won't spend cash. You are in a store and you find a couple of nice pantsuits, and you have a beautiful little credit card, so you charge. You don't think of it as being money spent. "I only spent $120 on clothes last year." That's right, plus you ran up a $400 bill at Penney's, on which you are paying $17 a month.

Next, compute your *forfeited savings.* For example, how much more does it cost you to eat because of buying convenience foods? You don't have time to bake or to fix meals that require much preparation. You must be able to get home, get the item out, put it in the oven or on the stove, and have it ready quickly.

Other forfeited savings result from not being able to spend time shopping in several stores to take advantage of all the bargains and sales. You also don't have time to make any clothes, raise a garden, make jelly and jam, can vegetables and fruits, or "do it yourself" on home and yard improvement projects.

Let's face it. A mother of several small children is already carrying a heavy work load. It is a full

---

*In most seminars, $9 is so low that I get booed for saying it.

time job being a wife and mother. One time when Meg was sick I had to stay home and take care of her and the kids for about three days. The second day I decided to be a top-notch homemaker and clean the kitchen. I scrubbed down all the cupboards. I took everything off the shelves, cleaned all the shelves and restacked them, cleaned the walls, got down on my hands and knees to scrub the floor, and really cleaned that kitchen. It took me four and a half hours.

I still had some energy left, so I decided to clean up the bathroom. I couldn't have been in that bathroom more than seven minutes when I heard this faint little tinkle, tinkle, clunk. I said to myself, "That is a funny little sound." I looked around the corner, and I didn't see anything, so I walked on out to the kitchen. There was our No. 2 son, George—then about three years old—right in the middle of his own kitchen rearranging project. He had flour, sugar, pots, pans, Comet, Vano starch, cornflakes, cereal boxes, dishes, and dog food strewn on the floor. How he did all that with a lousy little tinkle, tinkle, clunk, I'll never know! It took me forty-five minutes to clean up that mess; meanwhile he was destroying the bathroom.

Taking care of a family is a full-time job. If a mother holds down another job outside the home as well, you just have to figure a considerable sum will be lost in forfeited savings. I estimate it at $22 a week.

Next, how much extra will you spend at the *hairdresser's*? A lot of working girls say they never use a hairdresser; others overuse them. When I was working for the State of Oregon, a girl worked there who had two appointments every week. When she started working, she intended to work for seven months to get enough money to buy a freezer. That was eighteen years ago, and she has been working ever since. She says she works full time and brings home a good wage for the family, and her hairdressing money is part of her reward for bringing home that wage. Let's say that on the average, this item comes to about $6 a week.

Then, there is an interesting expense which we will call *"I Owe It to Myself."* Listen, Mom, *you do,* carrying your work load. I don't care how understanding your husband tries to be, he never fully understands. Only you know what you have to go through all day long, the pressures that are on you, from trying to run a home and a "career" at the same time. Your husband holds down one job, like other men do, but you hold down three jobs, and you owe it to yourself to splurge just a little bit once in a while. In that frame of mind you notice a beautiful $48 pantsuit on sale for $22.95. So you buy it. How do you justify it? "I owe it to myself." Yes, you do—and that expense is going to average about $4 a week.

Employment expenses: This is a catch all for employees association expenses, contributions to health insurance, office collections for everything from a gift for the boss to a handout for Eileen's cousin Fred, whose house burned down. Figure $3.50 a week.

Child care costs, assuming you have two children, will be about $75.00*a week. That comes out to $15.00 a day. Some babysitters charge as little as $7 a day for one child, and some will take two children for as little as $12 a day. But for two children $75 a week is probably what you will have to plan on paying.

There is a final expense for which I don't have a label; nor can I assign a cost to it. *What kind of dollar figure do I assign when I allow someone*

---

*I'm working with a mother in San Jose, California. The cheapest care she can find for her 2- and 4-year-olds is $600 per month.

else to raise my children? God has a priority system, remember? Our relationship to God comes first, then our relationship to our family, then our ministry, then our job. Here we are assigning someone else our no. 2 priority while we take care of no. 4. I don't know what dollar figure to put down for this. What will that ultimately cost us?

I used to think that if at the end of my life, I could point to two cars, a big house, membership in the right country club—all of the status symbols— I could look back and say I had a successful life. No more. If I end my life sitting on a welfare front porch in a borrowed rocking chair, and somebody comes to me and says, "What a joy it was to have your son [or daughter, or grandson, or granddaughter] over to see us. What a tremendous witness he is for the Lord! How alive and beautiful he is!" I'll be the richest man in the world.

What dollar figure do you put down for all of those things you miss out on by not being there when your children begin asking questions and giving answers?

I had (past tense, thank the Lord) a temper, my dad had a temper, and all of a sudden I began seeing temper manifest in the lives of my children. Scripturally, the sins of the father are visited unto the third and fourth generations, I said, "No, Lord, that's it; I am going to break the chain right here. I am not going to allow temper to be manifested in my life, and I am not going to have it manifested in the lives of my children." So the Lord has delivered me from temper, and I am now working with my children in this area.

Can you imagine me saying to a babysitter, "Listen, at this time we are dealing with the children about anger. Now, if George gets upset and loses his temper, you get down on his level and explain what the Bible says about getting angry at your brother or sister. If he yells and screams, explain what the Bible says about keeping a low voice"?

Sunday afternoon is a Bible study time for our family. Right now we are studying the 46 ways of a fool, and 21 things that make a wise son. We go through these, list a couple of verses for each, and then talk about them. We are also trying to memorize some of the verses. Can I say to the baby-sitter, "Our memory verse this week is 1 Chronicles 6:19; drill him a couple of times during the day"?

What kind of babysitter will be raising your children? Chances are, she will not be a Christian. Most of them aren't. She will just be doing it for the money to augment her family income. She won't want to be hassled by your kids. She may be on the phone half the time. She may say, "Get out of here, kids; go watch TV." She doesn't care about them as you do.

I can't do a great deal of good by lecturing to a group; I may make a couple of points, and a few principles may seep into the consciousness of my hearers. But with my children I can have a tremendous influence. I can mold them. Through my positive teaching and example, I can make outstanding successful citizens out of each one of those three children. If by chance they do go astray, which won't happen, it will not be anybody's fault but my wife's and mine—mostly mine because I am the spiritual leader in my family. It won't be the school teacher's fault, it won't be the Sunday school teacher's fault, it won't be the Boy Scout leader's fault; it will be my fault. I am determined not to have that type of failure applied to my account. So what dollar figure could I put for having someone else raise my children?

What dollar figure compensates for not living near

enough to your children to experience their wisdom? What I have learned from my children is absolutely amazing. There is no way I could put a price on it.

My little girl is named Margaret Mary and we call her Gem. She was three years old when she looked up at me and said, "Daddy, I love you—and I love Mommy and I love Greggy and I love Georgie and I love everybody."

I thought, *Now I am going to give her a lesson: I am going to teach her that we are not to love one member of the family more than another.* "Gem, who do you love more than anybody?" I asked.

She said, "Oh, I think I love Jesus."

So Daddy got a lesson.

One day I was out in our yard and I overheard a conversation between our then 7-year-old son, George, and the man next door. "How come you are not a Christian?" George was asking.

"We *are* Christians," the man said.

"Well, I never see you go to church," George replied.

What kind of dollar figure do I put down for having someone else raise my children, for having the joy of watching them taken away from me?

I am in the process of writing an advertisement; it goes something like this: "Wanted, young women to be involved in motivational dynamic research, responsible for life patterns, domestic engineering, instruction in moral responsibility." That beautiful-sounding job description is of a mother, a house-wife. Take a look at that job, Mom. Consider the opportunity you have to minister, to mold your children, to be a dynamic forceful witness for Christ.

Okay, I believe there is no way to assign a dollar cost to letting someone else raise your children, but we can add up the other expenses a working mother incurs. They come to $281. You earned $250, so it cost you a net of $31 to go out and work—$31 more than you earned.

Obviously, you can't have that, so what is going to happen? You must cut expenses. Your mother lives with you, and she does the baby sitting. She also fixes your hair and does the shopping. She can shop better than you can anyhow; she knows all the tricks. She also makes all of your clothes. You never go out to dinner, and you carry a sack lunch to work. Your husband works right next door to your place of employment, so you ride with him. That way you have no extra transportation or parking costs. And maybe you don't tithe, and you cheat on your taxes.

Okay, now you are making a little extra money, but at *what cost*? Even cutting all the corners, the most that a wife can expect to add to family income with today's wage and price structure is somewhere between $20 and $175 a month maximum. Assuming the husband earns $18,000 a year, with the expenses listed, you would have to gross $1,278 a month to break even (this because of increased tithe and taxes using 1988 tax rates).

Make Money Working for Yourself

There is a better way for a mother to supplement the family income than by taking a job. In fact there are many ways to add to household finances that are right within the framework and the structure of being a housewife and mother. Proverbs 31 suggests several of these ways.

1. *Make merchandise.* "She seeketh wool, and flax, and worketh willingly with her hands.... She perceiveth that her merchandise is good" (vv. 13, 18).

Some women really enjoy making straw flowers,

shadow boxes, decoupage boards, and they make extra money at the same time. Or you could make desktop pencil holders. Take a vegetable can and make sure the top is all cleaned up so no sharp edges remain. Paint the can green or brown, and then add black antiquing. Then tol paint some flowers or an owl or a scene of a barn on the can. Cut a piece of green felt and glue it to the bottom of the can. For an investment of about 10 cents you have an item worth $3.

You could turn out like the guy who graduated last in his class from college. At the twenty-year reunion somebody says, "I wonder what happened to old Harvey. He was so slow he could hardly add two plus two. He flunked algebra five times, and they finally just let him out so they wouldn't be embarrassed about his flunking algebra again." They are all laughing about poor Harvey when a chauffer-driven Rolls Royce arrives. Out of the back comes Harvey.

Everybody goes up and claps him on the back. "Harvey, what happened? Wow, what is this?"

Harvey says, "Oh, man, I was so lucky. I happened on to an invention that costs me $5 to manufacture and I market it for $30. You would be surprised how that 6% adds up!"

You can form little Raggedy Ann and Andy dolls out of play dough. Paint them and mount them on boards, and you have a little set that sells for about $7.50. The cost to make them is about $3. Or make macrame belts. Buy the buckles on sale for 50¢ and the cord for about $1. You come out with an $8 to $10 item.

Making merchandise, if you have a talent in these areas, can make you money. If nothing else, your merchandise would make marvelous gifts every year for all those on your birthday and Christmas lists. Not only will you save money, but your gifts will be more meaningful if you make them yourself.

2. *Design clothes.* "She maketh herself coverings of tapestry; her clothing is silk and purple. . . . She maketh fine linen, and selleth it; and delivereth girdles unto the merchant" (vv. 22, 24). Remember, a lot of working girls out there are spending $468 a year on clothes, so why not sew for some of them on a continuing basis? You can save them money and add to your income without ever leaving your home. I know a couple of women who are doing this. By working four hours a day on the average, they are able to generate income of around $250 a month free and clear of expenses.

A mother can even make her children part of her team. They can take stitches out—when she blows it, for example. Children have a real capacity for being involved in this type of activity if you make it important. Spend a little time in sharing some Scripture with them and give them little stories; they will be involved in a project right along with you. Then, of course, you can also work during their naps.

3. *Make nutritious meals.* "She riseth also while it is yet night, and giveth meat to her household, and a portion to her maidens" (v. 15). A busy mother, especially a working mother, most likely does not have time to plan a week's menu and then read the papers, do comparison shopping, and discover the best buys. So what you could do is to make up a week's meal plan in advance; then mail out the next week's meal plan, plus a list of all the stores that have bargains on food, to a subscriber list. This service could save the working mother a lot of time and money. Now I have talked with quite a few moth-

ers who would be more than willing to spend $2 a week for that service. They would save three times that much each week in having the meals planned and being able to shop the bargains.

4. *Invest wisely.** "She considereth a field, and buyeth it" (v. 26). You can actually put money into a deal and turn a profit. I am not necessarily saying you should go into the stock market and become a broker, but you can make some excellent buys at garage sales and thrift stores, for example. What you need to do is be aware of the value of various items.

Let's mention some things that could be good investments. Canning jars with glass lids and wire tops sell now for anywhere from $3 to $10 each. The big blue jars with porcelain tops sell for $5 to $10. We accumulated four dozen of these old jars from various sources, about $140 worth.

Insulators can be worth $3 to $5 each depending on the color. White ones are not worth as much as those that show some purple.

Old Coca Cola trays sell for $5 each now. A friend of ours going through Arizona stopped at a little shop and discovered they had 42 old Coca Cola trays for sale at $1 each. She gave the shopkeeper $25 for the whole lot and came back and sold them to a buyer for $105 ($2.50 each). The buyer turned around and sold them for $5 each.

If you spot something of value and it is marked, say, at 25¢, are you being fair if you take the bargain and do not tell the sellers they have something worth far more than the asking price? The answer is yes. We are being fair in that situation for two reasons.

From a legal standpoint the principle is *caveat emptor* which means "let the buyer beware." The seller is assumed to know what he is selling. It is

*Some of these "collectables" have become very popular in the 80s and sell for 5 times as much as these 1975 prices.

the buyer that needs to beware. So from a legal standpoint you have no obligation.

From a moral standpoint, you will do a disservice if you tell them. Let me illustrate why. A gentleman and I walked into a garage sale and discovered six matching crystal glasses. These things were beautiful merchandise, but they had been sitting somewhere gathering dust for years and looked bad. They were priced at 50¢ each and were worth probably $7 each. My companion bought the set for $3 and as we were walking out, I heard one woman say to the other, "I told you we could get 50¢ for them" They were very pleased; they got every penny out of those things that they hoped to get. They had been getting no use out of the glasses, which were just gathering more dust and dirt. This way they did get money out of them and they were happy.

Suppose I had gone to those women and said, "Listen, I really don't know how to tell you, but those glasses you have back there marked 50¢ are cut crystal; they are worth at least $5 to $7 each." Would I have helped them? More likely they would have said, "Oh, no! We just sold seven like them. So we have given away $49! And what about that punch bowl we sold last week? Oh, no, Mildred! Do you realize we have given away real crystal?"

Then their minds would go back over all the things they had sold. Quickly they would hang up a sign, "Temporarily Closed Garage Sale"—while they ran around checking prices. How about this? Is this more? Is that enough?

So take your bargains where you find them.

5. *Direct sales.* (This and the following are not really found in Proverbs 31, but I believe they can be good sources of income for the housewife.) By direct sales, I mean selling products such as Avon

or Amway. My mom sold Avon when we children were young. She would park the car at the end of a block and leave my brother and me in the car while she went up and down the street. We would play games and fight and do whatever brothers or sisters do. We seemed to have come out okay. There was plenty of love in the family.

As for Amway, I am impressed by the character of the men involved with that organization. The president and vice president of Amway are both Christians, and the direct distributors are often very highly motivated Christian brothers and sisters. Selling Amway gives an opportunity not only to make money but also to witness to neighbors and friends concerning the Lord's work in your life.

A different type of sales opportunity which gives ample opportunity for Christian service but doesn't involve door-to-door work is the sales of Christian books through racks in secular stores and through home book parties. Successful Living, Inc., is, perhaps, the best known organization offering this type of business with a ministry, and a new organization, Right Time International, specializes in the home book party concept. Since each distributor or dealer is independent, he or she can control the amount of time spent away from home while making a good income from the time invested.

With any business that you conduct from your own home, there is an added benefit that I have not even mentioned yet—the tax break. Everyone of these money-making ventures that centers in your own home makes you eligible to deduct portions of your electricity costs, your heating and cooking, your telephone, your travel, and your car expenses.

6. *Babysitting.* I would like to recommend this because you are a Christian mother, and babysitting

will give you the opportunity to minister to young children. You may be the only Christian influence some of them ever have in their young lives. They may never go to Sunday school or church, and yet you have the opportunity to share with them Christian principles and to really work with them in the areas of character development and spiritual awareness.

One word of caution: check the laws in your area as to how many children you can care for without having to qualify as a day nursery. Probably you will want to care for only a couple of children and will not need to be concerned about this, but check to be sure.

If you want to add to the family income, then, or feel you absolutely need to whether you want to or not, give careful—and prayerful—consideration to all your alternatives. I think—and I hope—you will decide that for the mother of younger children especially, a full-time job outside the home costs too much. And there are better ways to beat the dollar crunch at your place.

1987—Since writing this book, we've added Gordon to our family. The oldest three range from 18 to 23 and are in college or on their own. Meg never worked outside the home and the kids are a tribute to Meg's love and support of Mom at home. At seven, Gordon has 11 years of careful training and love ahead of him. I highly recommend you do everything possible to live on one income.

12

Training Children in Money Matters*

Suppose your child were to ask you, "Dad, Mom, what is heaven like?"

Do you know what your answer should be? "Heaven is like your home!" That's right, the love and harmony and respect and concern for one another in our homes should cause them to resemble heaven. I am afraid that here a lot of Christian homes fall far short.

Can you imagine the Father and the Son up in heaven arguing over something? Of course not. Heaven is all love and harmony. That's the type of home we should make for our children.

When our children ask us something, our aim should be to say yes. I am not suggesting that you give them everything they ask. But try to say yes, because that's the way our heavenly Father is. He always says yes unless there's some compelling reason to say no, and even then He does not simply say no. He tries to get me to think things through myself.

When you're right in the middle of doing the bills or something else requiring concentration, that's when one of your children will ask for something.

---

*See my book *Training Your Children to Handle Money* for a much broader discussion.

"Dad, can we go roller skating?"

"No."

You don't even think about it; you just say no. Then you may begin to reflect, *Why can't we go roller skating? I'll have time later this afternoon. I guess we could go roller skating.*

Instead of immediately saying no to your children, think about it.

Suppose it's a Sunday afternoon. "Dad, can we go out and play with Sean and Natalia in the front yard?"

That is against our rules. Sunday is a family day, and maybe we don't always spend it together, but we don't run around and make noise and tear up the neighborhood. God rested on the seventh day, and I want to allow our neighbors the same privilege.

If my boy comes on Sunday and asks to play with Sean and Natalia, I don't say no. I say, "Well, what is our rule on Sunday?"

"We stay home and play in the backyard only, with no friends."

"Is today Sunday?"

"Today is Sunday."

"Well, what do you think the answer is?"

"I guess we can't play with our friends."

I didn't say no. I encouraged him to make the correct decision.

It takes time to get over the automatic-no habit. The other day I was doing some work on taxes and my son said, "Dad, can you get a record for me?" I said no. I didn't even think. But then I stopped and said, "Wait a second. Okay, I'll come right now." He just wanted a record for his record player. We had some old records which I got from downstairs and let him have to play. I went back upstairs and, you know, he didn't bother me the rest of the evening. If I had said no, he would have been back twenty minutes later asking for something else.

There is a principle here. You see, my son was actually looking for me to respond to him. He was saying, "Dad, do you love me? Can you do something for me?" When we take time to respond to our children, they are happy.

We are the image of God to our children. If we can't meet their needs, they may conclude that we have a pretty poor God.

If you must say no to your children, never say no because "we can't afford it." That is not an acceptable answer. It is too much like saying, "Our God is either poor or stingy, and He doesn't give us enough money to go out and buy you a bike like Mr. and Mrs. Jones down the street did for their son."

My son says, "Daddy, can we buy a bike? I want a bike."

"Well, Honey," I reply, "do you really want a bike?"

"Yes, I really do."

"Why?"

"Sean got one. Paul got one."

I say, "That's fine, I think you should have a bike and there is no reason you shouldn't. I'll tell you what. You begin saving your money. If you save $1 this week, I'll put $1 into the bike fund too. I'll match every penny you save. When we get enough money to buy that bike, we'll go down and get it."

Perhaps I can't afford to go out and spend $40 to $60 for a bike, but I know that out of my budget I can probably match his 15¢ or 25¢ a week. If he really gets industrious and begins to work for a bike, that's tremendous. You have just taught him that he needs to work for what he wants. Out of the money he earns, he is going to tithe some, and is going to expect God to give him an increase. You can definitely afford a bike, the purchase of which will teach many valuable lessons to your child.

Dr. James Dobson in his book *Dare to Discipline* provides a most creative chart* of fourteen duties to require of children each day.

In our household we pay our children one cent a day for performing each of these duties properly. In a week they can earn 98¢ that way. Of course, if the child fails in one duty on a given day, he only receives 13¢ that day, and so on. If he misses on four things, however, he doesn't get any money. So he has to maintain a high performance level.

One of the toughest duties is to be nice to brother. One evening we were reviewing Greg's chart and got down to "be nice to my brother." He had really been nice to his brother all day long, but he hadn't brushed his teeth after meals without being told and had goofed up cleaning his room. He missed on four duties. "Oh, no!" he said, "I was nice to George all day for nothing!"

We need to teach responsibility to our children, and using the duty chart is one way to do it. Another way is to bring them in on family decision-making. When setting up the annual budget, for example, we might ask the children where they would like to go for vacation. Suppose they say Disneyland. Fine. We budget for gasoline and the other expenses. Then we establish a vacation bottle. The children know if they put extra money in the bottle, it will mean another ride at Disneyland or a side trip to Knotts Berry Farm or to Seaworld. Now they are

---

*Chart taken from the book, *Dare to Discipline* by James Dobson, Ph.D., copyright © 1970 by Tyndale House Publishers, Wheaton, Ill. All rights reserved. Used by permission.

"My Jobs"

November	14	15	16	17	18	19	20	21	22	23	24	25	26	27	28	29	30
1. I brushed my teeth without being told																	
2. I straightened my room before bedtime																	
3. I picked up my clothes without being told																	
4. I fed the fish without being told																	
5. I emptied the trash without being told																	
6. I minded Mommie today																	
7. I minded Daddy today																	
8. I said my prayers tonight																	
9. I was kind to little brother Billy today																	
10. I took my vitamin pill																	
11. I said "thank you" and "please" today																	
12. I went to bed last night without complaining . . .																	
13. I gave clean water to the dog today																	
14. I washed my hands and came to the table when called																	
TOTAL:																	

a part of the action. Then one day perhaps George says, "Daddy, can we buy a road race set?"

"George," I reply, "what's more important, having a road race set or having a great time at Disneyland? We are saving our money this year for Disneyland, aren't we?" You see, I didn't say no.

I want my children to know that God is sufficient to supply all needs. This idea of poverty being next to piety is not a Christian concept. God is one who delights in blessing His children.

At the same time, we need to teach children to be responsible in the use of all that God gives them. Remember, irresponsible use of resources was one of the seven major money mistakes cited in chapter 1. As mentioned there, Jesus taught that if we do well in using limited resources, we will receive more; but if we misuse what little we have, even that will be taken from us. The reason so many adults fail here is that they did not learn this principle in childhood. Responsible behavior enriches a person and irresponsible behavior impoverishes him. Hopefully, that message will get through and that valuable lesson will be learned by our children early.

We once gave our number-one son a Slinky for Christmas. If you are familiar with Slinkys, you know they have an average estimated life of about 3.2 minutes, right? They just have a way of getting all tangled up. But our son really began taking care of his Slinky. He saved it. He held off his brother and sister anytime they wanted to touch it. He really protected that thing. Six months later, he still had it. That pleased us so much that we got him a train for his birthday, because we knew he would take care of his things. The message: do well with what you have and you will receive more.

Then there are cases like my other son. You know

those indestructable Tonka toys? They're not. Neither are Fisher-Price toys, Fisher-Price has a one-year guarantee on all their toys. I expect to get a letter from them any time: "Please do us a favor; stop buying our products."

If I see one of the boys breaking a toy we've gotten him or tearing something apart, I don't feel that he should be given something else. When he asks for something, I may answer, "You didn't even take care of the _____ I gave you, so why should I give you more?"

That doesn't mean, of course, that I write off my son as "bad" and unworthy of another chance. He's a child, and he needs to learn right ways. Like me, he may be slow to learn some things. Just as my heavenly Father faithfully instructs me—sometimes teaching me by hard experience if I won't listen— so I must teach my children. That means my son may have to pay the price for his own irresponsibility by not receiving what he would otherwise. But after a while, of course, he does get another toy, another opportunity to learn responsibility.

The examples I have set down so far relate mostly to younger children. A similar reinforcement type of system can be continued into the teens. Of course, adjustments will be necessary. Somehow the incentive of a penny a day for performing duties begins to be inadequate about the time a child reaches junior high. He needs more than 98¢ a week earned allowance. So we need to increase the allowance system somewhat to take care of the additional needs of pre-teens and teenagers.

One thing I feel is absolutely essential in this system, and something I haven't yet pointed out, is that once the child gets his money (for our children, that maximum of 98¢), it doesn't mean he now has 98¢

to go out and spend on anything he wants. We are trying to teach the children responsibility not only in earning money but in spending it.

First of all, we teach our children the principle of tithing, giving 10% to God. So, a dime each week goes into the church offering on Sunday morning. In addition, we have taught our children that they need to be in a position to buy presents for other family members at special times such as Christmas. We have them save 10¢ each week for this purpose. (We also provide opportunities for them during the year to earn extra money to spend at Christmastime.)

If our children are saving for something special (in our family it's bicycles for each of the children), they put 25¢ a week into that fund.

A certain amount of money, though, is theirs to do with as they wish. If they want to blow it all on candy, if they want to save it, if they want to give it away, it is their choice. They have earned it, and they can spend it.

However, we monitor very carefully how they spend it and try to give them input. Was this right? Did you get value for that? We try to teach them to get their money's worth.

After living with this system for a number of years, by the time they reach junior high our children should be able to take substantial responsibility. I recommend that older children handle the responsibility for some of their personal needs. If your child eats lunch every day at school, rather than dole out 50¢ a day to him, put him on a regular paycheck. You may be receiving your income monthly, bimonthly, or weekly, so set it up the same for him. Give him all his lunch money for the designated period. If he is to get a haircut every six weeks or she is to have her hair done once a month, or whatever, give them that money in advance too. If school activities are coming up during that period, include the necessary funds for those activities. In other words, give the child a sum to cover all his anticipated expenses for a given period and let him be responsible for managing the money.

Someone is saying, "Oh, wow, if I ever gave Junior all of his money two weeks before he was supposed to spend it, by the third day, it would all be gone on candy."

If that is the case, let him learn a very valuable lesson during that two-week period. Since he won't have any money for lunches, he'll just have to do without lunch. Since he did not have his hair cut, he will face a corrective action. Since he has no money for the school trip, he will not be able to go. In other words, spending all one's money on candy has unpleasant natural consequences, and he may as well learn that right now.

It's very important that we allow our children to make a few mistakes with their money and to learn early the consequences of financial mismanagement. If the child can learn these lessons early in life, he will be saved many painful experiences as an adult.

One of the many things I can thank my parents for is teaching me early in life that I am responsible when I do wrong; I am responsible to make sure that some things go right.

If I did not have the money to get my hair cut in a timely manner, then Mom and Dad dipped into some of my other savings for it, or provided an appropriate restrictive or corrective action. One time Mom threatened to cut my hair herself. That almost devastated me, because I was sure she couldn't even begin to handle my precious hair. I learned very quickly to set certain funds aside and keep them for particular needs, to have money for the school trip or so I could go to the play when the time came, for example.

Sit down with your children periodically, survey the needs coming up, and designate chores or jobs for them to do to earn their allowance. I use the word *allowance* to mean that paycheck the children receive for performing their duties.

Many parents object to "earned allowances." They say, "There are certain things my children do around the house; they don't receive any allowance for doing these duties; they are expected to do them because they're part of the family. Their allowance, if they get one, is something else; it's not related to performance."

I can't quite accept that concept. One thing I want to teach my children about the society we live in is that we don't receive anything free; we work for what we receive. On the other hand, if we work we should certainly expect to benefit. As the Living Bible puts it, "Those who do the plowing and threshing should expect some share of the harvest" (1 Cor. 9:10).

Our whole economic system is based on barter: I give up some of my time in order to earn money; you give up some of your time to earn money. That money is our medium of exchange. I use the money I earn to buy the commodity you gave up your time to make. In exchange you buy the commodity I gave up my time to make.

We could do the same thing without money. I could come to you and say, "If you will construct an addition to my house, I will take care of your accounting for four years." We could trade back and forth like that, but money seems to be a more efficient way of handling the many complex transactions involved in modern living.

That being the case, I want my children to understand this system, to learn how to make it work to their benefit. This entails teaching them early in life that they will receive compensation for satisfactory performance, and there will be a withholding of that compensation or corrective action for nonperformance.

If your attitude has been one of just expecting the children to do things around the house, think it over. How do you handle the cost of his summer camp? You say that because he is part of the family the cost of camp is your responsibility and you will pay it. I see it somewhat differently. My boys go to camp each summer because they have performed many jobs during the year specifically to earn that right. It's not just a gift. You know, we appreciate what we have worked for much more than that which is given to us.

The basic principle behind all I've been saying here is that we need to prepare our children to live in the world as it really is. If they learn at home that industry and responsibility bring rewards while laziness and irresponsibility bring difficulties, they will have taken a giant step toward responsible Christian adulthood.

13

Who Gets Your Assets When You Die?

Before I became a Christian I didn't like to go to funerals. Death meant the end, *finis*; it was all over. Recently I had the opportunity to go to a glorious Christian funeral. What a time of celebration! Here was an individual who had lived a full, rich life on earth and now had gone home to a great reward. Wonderful!

Naturally, we are going to miss departed friends; we enjoyed their fellowship. But they are with Jesus, and that's great.

I believe God wants us to plan for the distribution of our goods at our death. God called one rich farmer a fool—no doubt for several reasons—but partly because he hadn't faced the question of what was going to happen to all his goods when he died (see Luke 12:20).

Now, I'm still a young man and I plan to live to be 70 or 80 years old. God says its given to man to live threescore and ten years and for reasons of good health, fourscore (Ps. 90:10). I am also honoring my father and mother, so the number of my days will be long (Ex. 20:12; Eph. 6:1-3). Does that mean I should wait till I'm 69 years, 11 months, and 29 days old before I prepare for distribution of my goods at death?

Hardly, because I could die tomorrow. Balancing the seventy to eighty year life-expectancy established by Scripture is the equally biblical warning, "Boast not thyself of tomorrow, for thou knowest not what a day may bring forth" (Prov. 27:1). And James specifically warns us that we should temper all our plans with the acknowledgment that it is only "if the Lord will, we shall live and do this or that" (James 4:13-15).

I'm sure that Stephen obeyed his parents and trusted in God, but that didn't prevent his untimely death as the first Christian martyr. James was beheaded, the first of the Apostles to die. In fact the Apostle John was probably the only one of the twelve apostles who reached the age of seventy. (One valid reason for shortened life is completion of a ministry—being martyred for Christ.)

We make many preparations that we never intend to need. Do you carry a spare tire because you plan to have a flat? Do you keep a fire extinguisher handy because you intend to have a fire? No, you want to be prepared just in case the unexpected happens.

Now you cannot provide for your family as you should, in case of your untimely death, through any other means than a will.

Your Most Valuable Assets

You say, "But I have nothing. I don't even own a house. What do I need a will for?"

You have children, don't you? What could be more important? Your relationship to God comes first, and your family is second, ahead of all other considerations. Should anything happen to both you and your spouse, who would take care your children?

In your will you name a guardian for them.

If you die without a will, the court will appoint guardians for your children. Will the court say, "The deceased parents were faithful members of the church and they really loved the Lord. We know beyond a shadow of a doubt that they would want a Christian couple taking care of these children, so that is what we will find"?

No way. The court is going to say, first of all, "What relative wants the kids?" Then they will ask if these people are physically and financially able to take care of the children. That's all they are going to ask. They are not going to ask how good Christians they are. If no relative takes the children, chances are the court will put them into foster homes, probably separating them if there are three or more.

I don't know what would happen in our case. I imagine that both my parents and Meg's would want the kids. Her parents are beautiful Christians and I'd love to have my children live with them, but I doubt they have the physical capability to cope with my three darling monsters. My parents* probably have the capabilities to keep up with them, but they've raised their family already. So our wills name some close friends, a pastor and his wife, as guardians for our children.

There is a tremendous benefit overlooked by many in the godparents system. Godparents commit themselves before the church to be responsible for the spiritual life of the child should anything happen to the parents. They also pray for these children and exercise concern for them even while their parents are living.

Select a couple for whom you have great love and respect. Say "You have such a high place in our thinking that we want you to take care of our

---

*I wrote this before my parents commited their lives to Jesus. Meg's Dad and my Mom are now with the Lord.

children should anything happen to us." You have just paid that couple the highest possible compliment, and they will likely be happy to accept that responsibility. Now they will pray for your family; they will be concerned about your family; and that's good. This way the possible future guardians of your children already know them and are concerned for their total welfare. What an advantage!

Your Earthly Goods

How should you distribute your wealth when the Lord calls you home? Many Christian financial advisors teach that you should give a tenth to the Lord. Just as you have been tithing all your life, a tenth of your estate ought to go to the Lord.

Others say that since the Lord's work already got a tithe of your income as you were receiving it, there is no need now to give anything. There is a standard phrase to that effect in many wills. "Having been a member of _____ church for these years and loving the church dearly but having given during my lifetime, I have decided not to give anything now." (That's not quite the phraseology they use, but that's what it says in essence.)

If one could read between the lines, some of these wills would say something like, "That will teach the board of elders to oppose me!" There can be some real bitterness involved in this.

A tithe for the church? Nothing for the church? I take an entirely different view. What you should do is give it all to God. It's God's to begin with and you are just managing it. Give it back to God when you and your spouse are done with it.

You say, "What about our kids? I owe it to the children to give it to them." I have talked to many Christian sons and daughters and most have expressed the attitude, "Mom and Dad worked their whole lives, and they loved that missionary over in Africa [or that Bible school wherever, or that Indian work, or that Gospel broadcast, or their local church]. We just wish they would give it to them. We don't need it. God is taking care of us."

The exceptions to this that I think of are Christian sons and daughters with tremendous spiritual problems, exhibited in their negative attitudes and their inability to handle their own personal finances. Some are actually waiting for Mom and Dad to die so they can get theirs—a rather unchristian attitude, to say the least.

Now, if your sons and daughters are not Christians, the worst thing you can do is leave them your money. You are not going to help a non-Christian by giving him money. If he is an alcoholic, he will drink himself to death. If he has financial problems, they will get worse.

You say, "But if I leave something to him, he can at least get out of debt."

No, he won't get out of debt. He'll make a down-payment on a bigger boat or a bigger house or a more expensive car and end up just that much further in debt. I have never seen an inheritance help a family having problems. People who are not following biblical principles have their lives out of balance, so they wobble and vibrate. Giving them more money to get things out of balance is not going to solve anything.

I talked with one woman who had five sons and daughters, none of them Christians. She said, "I just want so much to leave my assets to the Lord."

I said, "Well, why don't we just establish a will and do that?"

"Well, I want to, but first I want to get the kids

together and talk to them. I don't want them upset and angry at the church because I gave the inheritance to the church. I want them to understand why I am doing that."

I tried to persuade her just to do it and explain later. But, no, the kids were coming in August, and she would talk to them then. Unfortunately she passed away before August, without a will. That meant the estate was automatically to be divided equally among the five children. The result: Number 3 is suing Number 1; Number 5 won't talk to anybody; they are all accusing the oldest of taking the best things and not properly distributing. Number 3 thinks that since the others all have good jobs while she is poor and has sickness in the family, the whole inheritance should be hers.

The total value of that estate was $7,500. Imagine that type of destruction in a family for $1,500 a piece!

You don't help a non-Christian by leaving him money. All you do is compound his problems. And if your children really love the Lord, they probably don't want you to leave your assets to them.

Of course, there can be exceptions. Let's say you are a farmer, and your son is working with you on the farm. You want to leave it all to God and yet you want your son to have the farm to continue to make a livelihood.

All right, put it in trust, with the trust owning all the land and the church owning the trust. Provide for the son to have a twenty-year purchase agreement to buy back the land from the church. That's a good idea. You had to buy it to begin with. You had to scrimp and save and pour out sweat to get started. Why shouldn't he? God gave you the power and ability to get it; let God give him some too.

That way you can give everything to God without cutting off your son.

If you have minor children, you leave everything in trust to the children with the guardians appointed as trustees. (If you're willing to trust them to take care of the children, they ought to be able to take care of the money!) If all the money has to be used for the children before they turn 21, fine; that's what it is there for. But provide that when the youngest child turns 21, the residue of the estate goes to God whether it's $1 or $1,000,000.

I feel strongly about this. You see, I had the opportunity to be raised in a rather affluent area. I had three friends who had large trust funds waiting for them to turn 21 or 25. It ruined all three. One is an alcoholic, the second is on his fifth marriage, and the third became a drug addict. When one is 16 years old and has $75,000 waiting for him at the age of 21, he doesn't listen to anybody. That amount seems like all the money in the world! It's going to buy an awful lot of fast cars, fast girls, trips to Europe or anywhere else you want to go, so why should you listen to the school teacher or guardian or anybody else trying to tell you that studies are important? You have $75,000 waiting for you!

And the amount doesn't really matter to a 16-year-old; $12,000 seems just as big.

I knew a Christian brother whose grandmother left a quarter-of-a-million-dollar trust fund for him. He was to get a third ($83,333) when he turned 28, another third at 31, and the final third at 34. Meantime he was receiving income every month from the trust. He got a check for $820 monthly whether he even got out of bed or not.

This brother said to me, "What's my initiative in life? What's the drive to get out and do anything?" He didn't have very expensive tastes and $820 a month was more than ample to take care of him. He said, "I have been involved with several different business interests, but I have no drive to succeed. In another eight months I am going to get my first $83,000 and what am I going to do with it?" Oh, we could all spend $83,000, but would it be spent properly? That was his question. He had given his life to the Lord and he wanted to live it properly.

I don't know whether he followed my advice or not, but I told him to instruct the trust company to keep his $820 per month in the trust, and when the $83,000 arrived he should loan it interest free to the Lord's work for ten years. During that time he should get completely on his own, earn his living, and learn some of the valuable lessons that we all need to learn as stewards. Then, after ten years, he would be in a much better position to handle his money rather than have it destroy him.

See, the point is that money can become a great destroyer. It can be a great enabler, too, but only if we have learned to handle it properly. I don't see any reason to establish a trust fund for a minor. I think it's a destructive thing rather than constructive.

I know I don't want my children to have that sort of temptation hanging over their heads. They all are going to know from the time they are old enough to comprehend that money will be there to take care of them, but they are not going to inherit a thing; it's all going to God. After all, it's not mine anyhow, and it's certainly not theirs; it belongs to God.

*Making Your Will**

Plan for distribution of your assets at death. You know, seven out of eight Americans die without a will, and that means some $400 million a year lost to probate costs. Do you think God's kingdom could use $400 million?

So prepare a will, or, rather, get an attorney to prepare a will for you. No one else is really qualified, and the cost is not that great—probably only about $60 to $125.

Laws governing wills vary from state to state, so you need an attorney to assure that your will is valid in the state in which you live. In Oregon, where I live, for a will to be valid it must be in writing, it must be signed at the bottom by the person making the will, it has to be signed by two witnesses, it must make provision for the children, and the wife must be designated to receive at least one-fourth of the estate. In other words, you cannot write your wife out of the will. It is impossible; you cannot legally do it. Some states require that the widow receive 1/3 or even 1/2 of the estate.

In the State of Oregon, a holographic will (one in your own handwriting) is not legal. It must be typed or printed.

We are talking about a legal system that can get extremely complicated. A number of forms may have to be filled out at the very beginning when someone dies. Immediately your safety deposit box becomes sealed. A representative from the state must attest to the value of the box. You have to change the

---

*Many changes have taken place in estate tax law since 1975. Review your will with a professional every 3 to 5 years.

bank accounts. You must establish, in certain cases, a federal identification number and state identification.

It's a good idea from an estate-planning standpoint and from a legal standpoint for a wife and a husband to have separate bank accounts as well as a joint account. Food money for the family could be transferred to the wife's account. She can then manage it. My wife finally convinced me of that. She kept telling me I was taking her food money and spending it on other things. "Not so!" I insisted. Then I started looking into it, and I was. I had been telling her she was getting $220 a month for food and the household, and she really wasn't. So we opened an account for her. Hers is the only signature on it. I can't sign her checks. I put household money once a month into her account; then she manages it. That's her responsibility and she does quite well.

I also transfer money to her to pay my life insurance premiums. My wife owns my life insurance policies, so she pays the premiums. It's an estate-planning technique. Life insurance proceeds are not subject to federal income tax, but they are taxable by the estate. However, if she is the owner of the policies and pays the premiums, the proceeds are not a part of my estate and are not taxable.

In the area of transferring of property, of estate planning, of receiving goods in inheritances, of selling assets and reinvesting that money, may I give you a valuable word of advice? Before you make any decisions, at least pick up the telephone and call your accountant. Give him a brief outline of what you are involved with and ask what the tax consequences are going to be. I get frequent calls like that. It takes me a whole two or three minutes to say what basically will happen. I have never charged for that type of phone call.

What I dislike is when people come in all fouled up because they have acted in the dark. One woman bought her father's house from his estate. She was to have simply inherited it. She wouldn't have had to pay any income tax, no estate tax, no tax of any kind. But somebody had told her she would be liable for taxes so, in working out a way around it, it ended up costing her much more.

Her misunderstanding was a common one. Many people think that if they sell a piece of property and reinvest the money they don't have to pay taxes on it. Not true. You always pay tax on a gain unless it is from the sale of your personal residence and then you buy another personal residence. (There are other very specific exceptions.)

Does estate planning seem complicated to you? Believe me, it *is* complicated. I haven't even scratched the surface. That's why I insist that *in the area of estate planning, you need the help of professionals.*

When is the time to start? Anytime you want to do something with your estate that is beyond what the law will provide automatically. A young man, nineteen years of age, asked me, "Should I draw a will?"

I said, "Well, do you own anything?"

He said, "I have a car and about $2,000 in savings."

"What do you want done with it if something happens to you?"

"I would like half to go to the church, and half to go to Mom and Dad."

I said, "You need a will."

Now, if he had wanted it all to go to his parents, he wouldn't have needed a will because it would automatically go to them.

A safety deposit box is the best place to keep your will. Your attorney will also have a copy in his files. (I know one woman who keeps hers in her freezer. Talk about a safe place! In case of fire, her will is down at the bottom of the freezer where it is not likely to burn. She keeps all her important papers there. I call her two days before our appointments and tell her to thaw out the records, because we are going to review them!)

Well, as I said at the beginning of this chapter, I don't dread funerals anymore—at least not funerals of Christians. But sometimes I'm still a little sad. Too many who have prepared well for eternity haven't prepared at all for the estates they must leave behind. You won't leave us on that unhappy note, will you?

PART V

Avoiding Hidden Pitfalls

14

A Few Final Tips—But Oh, So Important

Whenever God says something, it's important, right? Well, then, if God says something not once or twice or even three times but *six times*, shouldn't we sit up and take notice?

Do Not Cosign

Six different passages in Proverbs warn us against being "surety" for another's debts (6:1-5; 11:15; 17:18; 20:16; 22:26-29; 27:13). Today we call that cosigning. I have one word of advice concerning cosigning: *Don't*. The Scripture is very explicit. "Be not thou one of them . . . that are sureties for debts." Then it goes on to explain one reason for this. "If thou hast nothing to pay, why should he take away thy bed from under thee?" (22:26-27).

Scripture not only warns against cosigning but does so in the strongest possible terms. It says the person who does this is "void of understanding" (17:18) and that he will "smart for it" (11:15). In fact, the Scripture teaches that if you are in such a position, having already cosigned, you should go to that individual, get down on your hands and knees, and beg him to let you out of that obligation.

Cosigning places you in a very dangerous position from many standpoints. For one thing it destroys relationships. I've known of several Christian couples who have been involved in cosigning notes for one another, and I have never seen the relationship survive unmarred.

I was with some friends once, talking with a credit manager of a hospital. He was insisting that my friends get a cosigner and borrow the money to pay their debt to the hospital.

I said, "Great, why don't you cosign for them?"

He said, "I wouldn't cosign for anybody."

I said, "Well, don't you find that just a little bit strange? I mean, you're insisting that they get a cosigner. Why don't you cosign for these people? They are nice people; don't you like them?"

He said, "I cosigned for a couple one time, and I'll never do it again. It completely destroyed our friendship."

The reason people usually need cosigners in the first place is that their financial management has been unsound. They are not going to change into responsible people just because you cosign for them. The tendency is to the contrary. You are making it possible for them to continue to be irresponsible. They are likely to default, which means you are likely to be stuck with the debt. That has a way of marring your friendly feelings toward them, to say the least. Or perhaps you will put pressure on them to pay, and that causes friction. Believe me, it just doesn't work out.

From a legal standpoint, cosigning is different from guaranteeing. A guarantor says that if the liable individual does not pay, and if you sue him and cannot recover everything due, then you can come after me for the money.

In contrast, the cosigner says that if the liable person does not make the payment when it is due, say the 14th, then on the 15th you may demand and collect the money from me. You have your choice, either him or me, but you do not have to exhaust any legal avenues trying to collect from the person who actually owes the money. So guaranteeing a debt is bad enough and cosigning is far worse.

Frequently I am asked, "How about cosigning for my son or daughter so that he or she can get ahead? After all, the children are just getting started in life, and how are they going to be able to buy anything on time and establish credit unless I cosign for them?"

Think through what you are saying. In effect, I hear you saying, "I want to teach my children early that God is not sufficient to meet their needs, that I am the one they are to look to for backing to buy their first car, get furniture, or lease a house."

Don't cosign. And if it seems awkward or difficult for you to refuse, just cite the Scripture. God plainly tells you there that you are not to do it, so how can you go ahead? Anyone who understands your commitment to obeying the Word of God ought to be able to understand that.

Get Counsel on Your Finances

The Bible says, "Where no counsel is, the people fall: but in the multitude of counsellors there is safety" (Prov. 11:14; see also 24:6).

You can go too far in this direction with the result that you get not only safety but confusion and stalemate. If you ask counsel of many people and then try to follow their advice, you will end up going in circles.

One of the purposes of counsel is to give you the

opportunity to see things from different perspectives. You don't get counsel with the idea of doing what someone else thinks you should.

For example, you may want to let a friend review your budget to see if it's realistic. This friend need not be a financial wizard of any sort. In fact, you may render the same kind of service to someone else. What you are doing is supplying a fresh outside perspective. You see, we have a tendency to lie to ourselves about matters, which, if we have to face them and defend them to somebody else, immediately appear to be absurd. So if you review someone else's budget, question items which seem to be non-essentials.

I questioned a loan payment on one man's family budget. "Man, the Lord really took care of us in that one," he said, and began to spin out the story. It summarized this way. They had an opportunity to buy a boat for which they didn't really have the money. It was a very good deal and they wanted it very badly, so they prayed and asked the Lord to protect them in the entire matter. They went to a loan company—no success. They went to another loan company with the same result. They went to a third loan company—no soap.

"Well, that's it, Lord," they said. "You are telling us that all doors are closed."

About an hour before they had to give their decision, one of the loan officers called back and said his company would lend the money after all. "Ah, it's a sign from God that He wants us to get it," they agreed.

The clincher was that they planned to use the boat to take the youth group for which they were co-advisors out water skiing. They would really minister with the boat.

So they got it—$65 a month. (They were, by the way, now coming out about $65 a month short of meeting their budget—a very interesting coincidence.) Almost immediately a problem developed inside the motor, and it wouldn't run. They had to order a part from the manufacturer—who put it on back order—and it was thirteen weeks before they were able to get the boat operational.

Meanwhile, because of pressures of business, they had stopped teaching their Sunday school class and attending the midweek meeting, but they were still going to Sunday church.

When they finally got the boat fixed, they were so excited about it that they decided to go away for the weekend. "Certainly nothing wrong with that," they told each other. "If we miss a few Sunday services, it is certainly not going to kill us." They had such a great time that he made a date to go again the next weekend and the weekend after that. Twelve weeks passed, and every weekend they were out with the boat.

See a problem?

We have to establish correct priorities in life: first, our relationship to God, second, our relationship to our families, third, our work, and a boat has got to be way down the list someplace.

As this man was describing his wonderful boat and how the Lord provided it, he stopped short and said, "You know, we have never taken that youth group in the boat yet. Never! That has to be the dumbest decision we have made in our lives. We could afford a boat like a hole in the head, and we should never have gotten it."

And I hadn't uttered a word of criticism.

As a result, he sold the boat. He took quite a loss on it because he owed $480 more than he was able to get for it. "That's it!" he said. "I've learned my lesson." He became active in the church, really living for the Lord again. Seven weeks later, you'll never guess what happened! Somebody *gave* him a boat. God had not been saying, "No, you can't have a boat." He was saying, "No, not now, not this boat."

You see? God does not begrudge us nice things; He just wants us to make sure our priorities are right.

Don't Put God in a Corner

You'll get all the boats, all the cars, all the nice things you will ever need. God will provide them. But we get ourselves in a trap. We say, "God, I really want that and if you don't provide it, I'll go down and borrow the money and you will have met the need by providing the way for me to borrow the money."

No, if He really wants us to have it and we really need it, He will give it His way, and that is not by incurring debts. Never put God in a financial corner by going into debt and calling it "buying on faith." God likes to provide the money in advance. Hudson Taylor said that God's work done in God's way will never lack for financial support. God is able to provide funds ahead of time as well as afterwards, and He much prefers to do the former. God is too wise to frustrate His purposes for lack of funds.

We probably don't dare say this to God, but the thought is there, "God I have this need, and if you don't provide for it by Friday, I have already got a cosigner and I can go down and get it myself."

What kind of faith is that? If you can assume debt, trusting God to provide the payments each and every month, why not trust God to provide all the money in advance?

I counseled a young woman who was on welfare. She not only couldn't afford monthly payments; she couldn't even afford car insurance. She had found a cosigner for a note to buy a car and she wanted me to tell her I thought it all right for her to sign a contract for $42 a month.

She needed the car; there was no question about that. Her old car was hardly fit for the junkyard. I urged her to trust God rather than incurring a debt she could not pay.

"But I have to have a car," she said. "Nobody is going to give me one!"

"Give God a chance," I urged. "At least wait one week so He has time to work."

You know what happened? Somebody gave her a car. (I have given one car away three times now. I just say, "It's yours until you are done using it, and then find somebody else who needs it and let me know who has it." It's now on to its third driver. Praise the Lord! I wasn't using it; I didn't need it.)

One individual to whom we intended to give this car went out and bought a car "on faith" that God would provide the money. And he did—after a fashion. But her payments were frequently late, which meant late charges on top of the high interest she was already paying. Besides that, the car never did run right. She probably spent $500 in repairs on that car in a year. You know how much money we spent that year for repairs on the little car we were going to give her? None. God had it all worked out—a car that would have cost nothing for repairs, and no monthly payments, to give her a chance to build up some savings so she could buy a better car for cash in a year or so! But she blew it.

If we put God into a financial corner by buying on credit, we don't give Him a chance to work out alternatives.

What really brought this home to me was an experience with Greg, our oldest boy. His school was staging a white elephant sale, and the class bringing in the most items to sell was to get a prize. I learned indirectly that Greg was telling everybody in the class that he was going to collect so many white elephants that we would have to haul them all down there in the back of the station wagon. I went home and told Meg, and it was all news to her. So we called Greg to an accounting. "You cannot obligate us like this," we said. "You can't go out and tell people we are going to do something without checking with us first."

"Well," he replied, "I just knew you would help 'cause you have always helped me before and I knew you wouldn't let me down."

What are you going to do with trust like that?

We took a privilege away from him for Saturday to let him know he had violated one of our principles. Then we stayed up until after midnight searching through closets and the garage to fill the back of the station wagon with white elephants.

I think that's the way God is. We mess things up, and He says, "I am going to take care of you, but I am also going to let this or that happen to try to catch your attention, to let you understand you haven't quite got the right principle established."

Why not have money set aside ahead of time to buy a car for cash? But don't just go out and buy. Say, "God, I need a new car. You could provide a car for me, in which case you tell me what to do with the $3,000. If you don't provide by Friday, I'll gather that I'm to go out and buy one."

That would be terrific! God might be so pleased He would get you a fine car, and then tell you what to do with the $3,000.

Learn Simple Skills

There is no need for you to be a Helpless Hannah and to pay someone a big service charge for simple tasks around the house that you can learn to do yourself. I have a book that tells how to make simple household repairs, and it has saved me a lot of money.

One day our TV stopped working, so I went to the book, opened to the index, and found the television section. I read, "If your TV is not working, under no circumstances try to repair it."

Now that's good advice. I was sitting at Mom's once watching a TV repair man work on a color set. He got his screwdriver in there and was tinkering around and all of a sudden he did a dive through the air with a full twist and a back flip up against the cupboards. "Boy, I know better than that!" he said.

If you know better than that and still get shocked, I sure am not going to put a screwdriver in there, I thought. So, be careful in attempting home repairs, because if you don't know what you are doing, you can really hurt yourself.

Even so, before you call a repair man, check some things. My home repair book said to first plug in the TV. That's pretty obvious, but every repair man can tell you stories of being called out to repair TVs, radios, or appliances that have simply been unplugged. Maybe the vacuum cleaner wand caught the cord, or a pet or child pulled it, or it just worked loose. So check to be sure it's plugged in; it could save you an embarrassing and expensive house call.

Next, turn it on and note whether the lights in the back of the set are on, my book said.

No, the lights were not on.

Check to see if your fuses are burned out, was

the next instruction. I went to the breaker box to see if any of the safety breakers had flipped off. They hadn't, so I read the next sentence: check to see if the plug is working by plugging in another appliance. I plugged in another appliance, and it worked fine.

I went down to the next instruction: check to see if the cord has become frayed, or the plug-in damaged. I looked and, sure enough, my Tarzan in unplugging the TV had managed to pull one of the wires off the prong. I carefully took my screwdriver and fixed it, and the lights in the back of the set came on. I had saved myself a house call.

Not only had I saved a house call—$12 or $14—but the serviceman would have tested all the tubes because he was there anyway, and he would certainly have found three or four weak tubes, and it would probably have cost me $20 or more.

Develop some self-reliance. Not only will it save you money, but you will feel good about being able to "do it yourself."

Be a Good Witness

Finally, handle your financial affairs in a way that is honoring to the Lord Jesus Christ, whom you represent. That means, of course, that you must be prompt in meeting your obligations. What kind of witness is it to steal (not pay your just debts) or to lie (not pay when you agreed—on the due date)?

Beyond that, your entire financial situation reflects on or enhances your witness. That doesn't mean you have to be rich to be a good witness for Christ, though in some situations affluence certainly does open doors and enhance one's witness.

For example, George Otis has a ministry to wealthy and influential people. Picture George Otis as he talks with the president of a multi-million dollar corporation, a man whose salary is say, $120,000 a year. George says, "You really ought to turn your life over to Jesus because He meets needs and takes care of His children. Come on out and get into my '58 Wreckmobile and I'll drive you down to the Whatzit Burger for lunch so we can talk about how great God is."

Do you think that would enhance George's witness?

In his book *What Did Jesus Say About That?* which I mentioned earlier, Stanley Baldwin describes an actual case of a woman who gave away everything and lived in poverty with the misguided notion that she was pleasing the Lord.

> When I was growing up in a sawmill town in Central Oregon, I often saw on the streets an old woman we called the Carrot Queen. She was an impoverished widow who kept herself alive by peddling carrots and other vegetables from her small garden. I can still see her in my mind's eye, shabbily dressed, shuffling along the sidewalk, pulling a child's wagon with her produce in it. Along with the carrots, she peddled religion whenever she had the chance.
>
> The story around town was that she would not have had to live as she did. When her husband died, he left adequate provision for her. But "that so-called church got it all." She had given everything away, and now was the town oddity.
>
> I don't know what Jesus thought about the situation. I don't know whether He commended her as He did the biblical widow or condemned the modern day counterparts of the Pharisees who devoured widow's houses (Matthew 23:14), or both. But I do know what her reputation was around town. It was bad. And I know what people thought of the religious group that had taken advantage of her. And that was bad.

It's sad that the "Carrot Queen" not only impoverished herself but was an unfavorable reflection on the very One she had meant to please and honor.

God wants you to be a witness for Him and a representation of how good and powerful and glorious He really is. Thus, generally speaking, the things that are for your good are also for His glory, and that includes material abundance.

I'm glad I serve such a God. Aren't you?

Malcolm MacGregor conducts seminars teaching these principles throughout the United States. If you would like to know when he is in your area, or if you are interested in sponsoring a seminar, write for information from:

> Your Money Matters
> 4618 SW Pacific Coast Hwy.
> Waldport, OR 97394

If you want a workable tool to help you implement the principles about which you have just read in this book, you can avail yourself of a book called *Financial Planning Guide for Your Money Matters*. It contains all the forms you will need to work out a budget, and additional hints on savings.